Michigan Cooks

C. S. MOTT CHILDREN'S HOSPITAL

This cookbook is a collection of favorite recipes,
which are not necessarily original recipes.

Published by The Regents of the University of Michigan,
a Michigan Constitutional Corporation,
the C. S. Mott Children's Hospital, and
The University of Michigan Health System

1522 Simpson Road East
Ann Arbor, Michigan 48109-0718
313-936-9836

Library of Congress Catalog Number: 96-86282

ISBN: 0-9652189-0-2

Designed, Edited and Manufactured by
Favorite Recipes® Press
P.O. Box 305142
Nashville, Tennessee 37230
1-800-358-0560

First Printing: 1996 15,000 copies

Book Design by Steve Newman

Contributor List

Robert and Kathryn Altman

Donna Auer

Jimmy Barrett

Frank Beaver

Carolyn Benson

Gordon "Red" and Joy Berenson

Christine Berry

Judy Bliss

Linda Bove

Michael Boyd

Jim Brandstatter

Kathy Brennan

Maggie Brownridge

Trudy Bulkley ("Mother Goose")

Mary Lou Butcher and Jack Casey

Rod and Sandra Campbell

Michele Capparelli-Tally

Lloyd and Laurie Carr

Anne Cavanaugh

Diane Chambre

John and Mary Lou Dasburg

Joe Diederich

Carol Dubritsky

Carol Ent

Sylvia Ertman

Nell Fallon

Jimmy Barrett

Trudy Bulkley

Contributors

Contributor List

Rod and Sandra Campbell

John and Mary Lou Dasburg

Contributors

Steve and Angie Fisher

Christine Gaucher

Dara Gaucher

Ellen and Steve Gaucher

Erica Gaucher

Kathy Gaucher

Edward Goldman

Joann Graham

Francis Grant

Suanne Grousett

Shari Hartley

Marilyn Hawkins

Jean Henrickson

Sara Hickey

Bob Hilty

Max Hodge

Susan John

Timothy Johnson, MD

Rob Jones

Ed and Juliette Jonna

Gail Kaufmann

Betty Kelsch

Sandy Kienow

Deborah Klinger

Steve and Kate Lambright

Barbara Lanese

Tonie Leeds

Brenda Livingston

Nancy Lyke

Dianne McNutt

Edna Miller

Susan Milne

Jody Misiak

Kathy Mount

Peter Murchie

Virginia Simpson Nelson, MD

Andrea Fischer Newman

Marylen Oberman

Lynn O'Neal

Kathy Prasol

Joe and Carolyn Roberson

Prue Rosenthal

Frances Rupp

Cindy Scheer

Bo and Cathy Schembechler

Rhonda Schoville

Kathleen McCormick Schulz

Raechelle Sedik

Diane Shember

Carol Spengler

Nicole Stanbridge

Judi Stanford

Deborah Klinger

Ed and Juliette Jonna

Contributors

Contributor List

Kathy Mount

Robbie Timmons

Bo and Cathy Schembechler

Contributors

Deborah Sullivan

Walter Szepelak

George Tattersfield

John Temple

Robbie Timmons

Cecilia Trudeau

Patricia Waller

Molly Walsh

Patricia Warner

Janice Warren

Rosanne Whitehouse

Trudy Widner

Therese Wion

Nellie Wolgast

Contents

C. S. Mott Children's Hospital:

There is no such thing as a typical day at C. S. Mott Children's Hospital. Every day is remarkable because on any given day hundreds of children—from infants to young adults—will receive health-restoring and often lifesaving treatments. They will suffer from common ailments and rare disorders, they will be the victims of accidents and viruses, congenital birth defects, and random illnesses.

But however different their physical circumstances may be, these young patients will all have one thing in common: the quality of care they receive will be the best available. They will be treated by some of the country's leading pediatric and surgical specialists. They will be under the care of highly trained nurses and nurse clinicians. They will have access to the most advanced treatments. They will benefit from the newest research discoveries in the care of pediatric patients. They will have the attention of teams of health care professionals: physicians, nurses, social workers, child life specialists, physical therapists, and many others.

They will also experience another, intensely personal dimension of care. From the moment they are greeted at the admissions desk, these youngsters and their families will know what it is to be in a welcoming environment designed specifically for their needs. Their comfort will be a major concern of everyone they meet. Nurses, social workers, physicians, physical therapists, and volunteers will all work together to provide the unique kind of child-centered, family-focused care that is standard practice at C. S. Mott Children's Hospital.

It is this combination of expertise and technology, knowledge and compassion, that has made C. S. Mott a leading center for children's health care in Michigan. Each year, we receive referrals from thousands of pediatricians, primary care physicians, and other practitioners throughout the state, the region, and the world. They know us by reputation and by the experiences of their patients. They know that there is no better place for children than C. S. Mott Children's Hospital—a hospital where children come first.

9

Cookbook Greetings from
Patricia A. Warner
Associate Hospital Director
Administrator—Mott Children's Hospital
University of Michigan Health System

Welcome to the world of Mott Children's Hospital. Our young patients, their families and all our staff appreciate your support of the Hospital through the purchase of *Michigan Cooks*.

This year marks two important milestones in the history of pediatric health care on the University of Michigan campus—the 25th anniversary of the Mott Children's Hospital and the 75th anniversary of the Department of Pediatrics. We are pleased that so many of our friends and supporters are celebrating with us by contributing their favorite recipes. We are grateful for their participation.

Enjoy the recipes and pictures and know that with the purchase of this cookbook you have joined so many others in supporting the finest care available for children and their families at one of the country's leading pediatric hospitals.

Thank you!

Patricia A. Warner

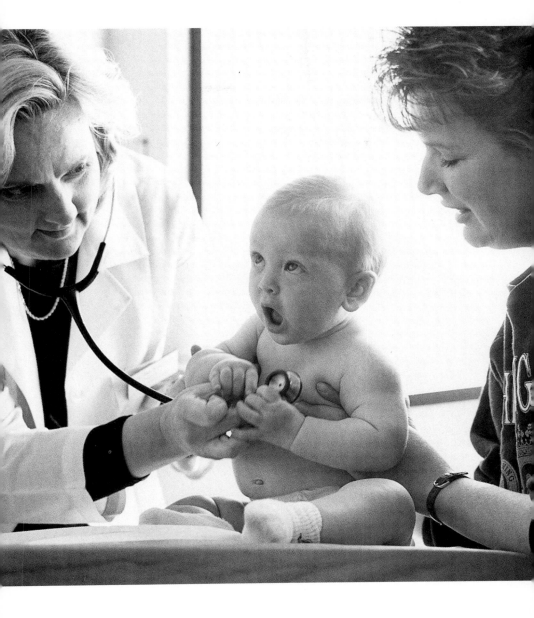

Appetizers & Soups

Bo and Cathy Schembechler

*For the past 25 years Bo has
taken the time to support our
hospital in a variety of ways.*

Mushroom Triangles

Sauté the onion in $1/4$ cup butter in a skillet until tender. Add the mushrooms. Sauté for 2 to 3 minutes. Add the garlic and madeira. Simmer until the liquid is reduced by half. Remove from the heat and cool slightly.

❖ Stir in the cream cheese, sour cream, parsley and egg yolk. Season with salt and pepper.

❖ Brush three sheets of the phyllo dough with melted butter. Stack the sheets and cut into 6 strips. Place 1 tablespoon of the mushroom mixture on the end of each strip. Fold up as for a flag, forming a triangle. Repeat with the remaining dough and mushroom mixture. Place on a baking sheet lined with buttered parchment paper.

❖ Bake at 350 degrees for 10 to 15 minutes or until golden brown. Serve immediately.

❖ Yield: 60 servings

Approx Per Serving:
Cal 52; Prot 1 g; Carbo 5 g; T Fat 3 g;
54% Calories from Fat; Chol 11 mg;
Fiber <1 g; Sod 60 mg

Bo and Cathy
Schembechler

$1/2$ cup chopped onion
$1/4$ cup butter
$1 1/2$ pounds mushrooms, chopped
2 cloves of garlic, minced
$1/3$ cup madeira or sherry
4 ounces cream cheese, softened
$1/2$ cup sour cream
2 tablespoons chopped parsley
1 egg yolk, beaten
Salt and pepper to taste
1 (16-ounce) package phyllo dough, thawed
$1/4$ cup melted butter

13

Appetizers & Soups

Spicy Almonds

Heat the peanut oil over medium-high heat in a heavy skillet. Add the almonds. Sprinkle with 1/2 cup of the sugar.

❖ Sauté until the almonds are golden brown and the sugar is caramelized.

❖ Toss the almonds with the salt, cumin, pepper flakes and remaining 1 tablespoon sugar in a bowl.

❖ Serve warm or at room temperature. Store in an airtight container.

❖ Yield: 16 (1-ounce) servings

Approx Per Serving:
Cal 156; Prot 4 g; Carbo 10 g; T Fat 12 g;
66% Calories from Fat; Chol 0 mg;
Fiber 2 g; Sod 202 mg

Susan Milne

3 tablespoons peanut oil
2 cups whole blanched
    almonds
1/2 cup sugar
1 1/2 teaspoons salt
2 1/2 teaspoons ground
    cumin
1 teaspoon hot pepper
    flakes
1 tablespoon sugar

15

Bar Cheese

Diane Shember

1 (16-ounce) package
    Velveeta cheese
1 (5-ounce) jar prepared
    horseradish
1/2 cup mayonnaise
1/4 cup wine or wine
    vinegar

Melt the cheese over low heat in a heavy saucepan, stirring frequently. Stir in the horseradish, mayonnaise and wine. Spoon into a chafing dish or serving bowl.

❖ Serve either warm as a dip, or chilled as a spread for crackers. May store in the refrigerator for weeks.

❖ Yield: 25 (1-ounce) servings

Approx Per Serving:
Cal 103; Prot 4 g; Carbo 1 g; T Fat 9 g;
79% Calories from Fat; Chol 20 mg;
Fiber <1 g; Sod 290 mg

16

Appetizers & Soups

Beer Salami

Combine the ground beef, Tender-Quick, garlic powder, pepper and hickory-smoked salt in a large bowl; mix well.

❖ Chill, covered, in the refrigerator for 5 days.

❖ Knead the mixture and shape into 3 logs. Place in a large baking pan.

❖ Bake at 150 degrees for 10 hours, draining pan drippings occasionally.

❖ Yield: 80 (1-ounce) servings

Approx Per Serving:
Cal 63; Prot 6 g; Carbo <1 g; T Fat 4 g; 58% Calories from Fat; Chol 21 mg; Fiber 0 g; Sod 372 mg

Diane Shember

5 pounds ground beef
5 tablespoons Tender-Quick
2 1/2 teaspoons garlic powder
2 teaspoons pepper
1 teaspoon hickory-smoked salt

17

Layered Taco Dip

Jody Misiak

3 ripe avocados, peeled
2 teaspoons lemon juice
1/2 cup mayonnaise
1/2 cup sour cream
1 envelope taco seasoning
   mix
1 (16-ounce) can refried
   beans
8 ounces Cheddar or
   Monterey Jack cheese,
   shredded
2 cups seeded chopped
   tomatoes
5 green onions with tops,
   chopped
1 (6-ounce) can sliced
   black olives, drained

Mash the avocados with the lemon juice in a small bowl until smooth; set aside.

❖ Combine the mayonnaise, sour cream and taco seasoning mix in a medium bowl, stirring well.

❖ Layer the beans, avocado mixture, sour cream mixture, cheese, tomatoes, green onions and olives in an 8x12-inch dish.

❖ Chill, covered, in the refrigerator. Let stand at room temperature for 15 minutes before serving. Serve with taco or nacho chips.

❖ Yield: 70 (1-ounce) servings

Approx Per Serving:
Cal 55; Prot 2 g; Carbo 3 g; T Fat 4 g;
69% Calories from Fat; Chol 5 mg;
Fiber 1 g; Sod 124 mg

18

Mix the beans with half the taco seasoning mix in a small bowl; set aside. Mix the remaining taco seasoning mix with the sour cream in a medium bowl. Mash the avocados with the lemon juice, onion, salt and pepper in a bowl.

❖ Layer the beans, avocado mixture, sour cream mixture, cheese, olives, tomatoes and green onions in a flat round glass dish.

❖ Serve with large tortilla chips.

❖ Yield: 78 (1-ounce) servings

Approx Per Serving:
Cal 43; Prot 1 g; Carbo 3 g; T Fat 3 g;
65% Calories from Fat; Chol 4 mg;
Fiber 1 g; Sod 97 mg

Sandy Kienow

1 (16-ounce) can refried
  beans
1 envelope taco seasoning
  mix
2 cups sour cream
3 ripe avocados, peeled
1 tablespoon lemon juice
1 tablespoon grated onion
Salt and pepper to taste
4 ounces Cheddar cheese,
  shredded
1 (6-ounce) jar black
  olives, drained
3 tomatoes, sliced
6 green onions, chopped

19

Chicken Soup

Andrea Fischer Newman

Vice President
Northwest Airlines
Regent of the
University of Michigan

1 (3-pound) chicken, cut
    into 8 pieces
2 large leeks
3 ribs celery with leaves
4 carrots
2 large parsnips
2 cloves of garlic, minced
1 tablespoon kosher salt
1/2 bunch fresh dill,
    chopped
1 bunch flat-leaf parsley,
    chopped

R inse the chicken and pat dry. Place in a large stockpot. Slice the leeks, celery, carrots and parsnips into halves lengthwise then crosswise. Place in the stockpot, adding water to cover. Add the garlic, salt, dill and parsley.

❖ Bring to a boil. Boil for 10 minutes; reduce the heat to low. Skim off the top.

❖ Simmer for 50 to 60 minutes, stirring occasionally.

❖ Remove the chicken and vegetables with a slotted spoon; let cool. Chop the chicken, discarding skin and bones. Slice the vegetables into bite-sized pieces. Return the chicken and vegetables to the broth.

❖ Simmer until heated through. Ladle into serving bowls. May store in the refrigerator or freezer.

❖ Yield: 8 servings

Approx Per Serving:
Cal 238; Prot 27 g; Carbo 18 g; T Fat 7 g;
25% Calories from Fat; Chol 75 mg;
Fiber 5 g; Sod 914 mg

20

Appetizers & Soups

Coach Carr has continued in the tradition of other Michigan football coaches by supporting our hospital.

Lloyd and Laurie Carr

1¹/₂ pounds ground beef
2 cups sliced onions
1 cup chopped celery
2¹/₂ tablespoons chili
    powder
¹/₂ cup water
Garlic powder to taste
2 (28-ounce) cans stewed
    tomatoes
2 teaspoons salt
Tabasco sauce to taste
1 tablespoon sugar
1 tablespoon
    Worcestershire sauce
1 (28-ounce) can red
    kidney beans, drained
1 (28-ounce) can hot chili
    beans, drained

Brown the ground beef, onions and celery in a large heavy 8-quart saucepan, stirring until the ground beef is crumbly.

❖ Mix the chili powder with the water. Add to the ground beef with the garlic powder, tomatoes, salt, Tabasco sauce, sugar and Worcestershire sauce.

❖ Simmer for 45 minutes, stirring occasionally. Add the kidney beans and chili beans.

❖ Simmer for 20 minutes longer, stirring frequently.

❖ Yield: 8 servings

Approx Per Serving:
Cal 449; Prot 31 g; Carbo 52 g; T Fat 13 g;
26% Calories from Fat; Chol 63 mg;
Fiber 17 g; Sod 1884 mg

21

Cincinnati Chili

Prue Rosenthal

1 1/2 teaspoons salt
1 pound ground beef
2 onions, chopped
2 cloves of garlic, minced
1 cup tomato sauce
2 tablespoons catsup
1 cup water
1 tablespoon red wine
    vinegar
1 tablespoon chili powder
1 tablespoon paprika
1 teaspoon pepper
1/2 teaspoon each cumin,
    turmeric, marjoram,
    allspice and cinnamon
1/4 teaspoon each
    nutmeg, cloves,
    mace, coriander
    and cardamom
1/2 bay leaf
1 teaspoon honey
1/2 ounce unsweetened
    chocolate, or to taste
1 (16-ounce) can kidney
    beans
1/2 to 1 cup tomato juice
12 ounces shredded
    Cheddar cheese

Prue, along with Linda Bove, has made the Annual Save-a-Heart Fund-raiser a huge success.

Sprinkle 1/2 teaspoon of the salt in a large skillet. Add the ground beef, onions and garlic. Cook over medium heat until the ground beef is browned but still soft.

❖ Add the tomato sauce, catsup, water and vinegar. Bring just to a boil. Add remaining 1 teaspoon salt, chili powder, paprika, pepper, cumin, turmeric, marjoram, allspice, cinnamon, nutmeg, cloves, mace, coriander, cardamom, bay leaf, honey and chocolate. Add the beans and mix well.

❖ Simmer, covered, over very low heat for 1 hour, adding the tomato juice as needed; the chili should be thick. Discard the bay leaf.

❖ Ladle into bowls. Sprinkle with the cheese.

❖ Yield: 6 servings

Approx Per Serving:
Cal 513; Prot 37 g; Carbo 26 g; T Fat 30 g;
52% Calories from Fat; Chol 116 mg;
Fiber 8 g; Sod 1652 mg

22

Idaho Wild Rice and Mushroom Soup

Rinse the rice under cold water until the water runs clear; drain. Bring salted water to a boil in a saucepan. Add the rice. Simmer, covered, for 35 minutes or until tender; drain well and set aside.

❖ Sauté the onion in the butter in a large kettle until tender but not browned. Add the wild mushrooms, white mushrooms and celery. Sauté until tender.

❖ Stir in the flour gradually. Cook over low heat for 3 minutes, stirring constantly.

❖ Add the broth, rice, curry powder, dry mustard, thyme and white pepper. Bring to a boil. Boil for 5 minutes, stirring constantly; reduce the heat.

❖ Stir in the sherry. Simmer for 5 minutes, stirring occasionally.

❖ Ladle into serving bowls. Sprinkle with the parsley.

❖ Yield: 6 servings

Approx Per Serving:
Cal 250; Prot 10 g; Carbo 30 g; T Fat 10 g;
34% Calories from Fat; Chol 21 mg;
Fiber 1 g; Sod 793 mg

Prue Rosenthal

1 cup wild rice
Salt to taste
1 onion, chopped
1/4 cup unsalted butter
1 cup chopped wild
    mushrooms (shiitake,
    morels)
1 cup sliced white
    mushrooms
1/2 cup thinly sliced celery
1/4 cup flour
6 cups chicken broth
1 teaspoon curry powder
1/2 teaspoon dry mustard
1/4 teaspoon thyme, or to
    taste
1/2 teaspoon white pepper
1/3 cup sherry
1/4 cup fresh parsley
    leaves

23

Salmon Chowder

Christine Gaucher

8 ounces potatoes, peeled,
    cut into 1/4-inch cubes
1/4 teaspoon salt
2 1/2 cups milk
3/4 cup minced onions
2 tablespoons unsalted
    butter
1 tablespoon flour
1 (8-ounce) salmon steak,
    skinned, boned
2 ounces smoked salmon
2 tablespoons chopped
    fresh dill, or 2
    teaspoons dried dill
1 tablespoon lemon juice

Combine the potatoes, salt and milk in a saucepan.

❖ Bring to a boil; reduce heat. Simmer for 10 minutes, stirring frequently.

❖ Sauté the onions in butter in a small skillet until tender. Sprinkle with the flour, stirring to blend. Simmer for 3 minutes.

❖ Stir the onions into the potato mixture. Simmer for 5 minutes, whisking frequently.

❖ Place the salmon steak in a heavy skillet. Cover the top side of the salmon steak with buttered waxed paper. Cook, covered, for 8 to 10 minutes, turning once. Uncover the skillet and remove waxed paper. Transfer the salmon steak to a warmed plate. Break into bite-size pieces.

❖ Break up the smoked salmon into bite-size pieces. Add to the potato mixture. Add the salmon steak pieces, dill and lemon juice. Simmer until heated through, stirring constantly.

❖ Yield: 4 servings

Approx Per Serving:
Cal 331; Prot 22 g; Carbo 24 g; T Fat 17 g; 45% Calories from Fat; Chol 79 mg; Fiber 1 g; Sod 353 mg

24

Linda, along with Prue Rosenthal, has made the Annual Save-a-Heart Fund-raiser a huge success.

Place the turkey carcass in a stockpot with water to cover. Add salt and onion flakes. Simmer for 1 to 2 hours; let stand until cool.

❖ Remove any turkey from the carcass and reserve, discarding bones. Set aside in the refrigerator. Strain the broth into a large saucepan.

❖ Sauté the onion in the oil in a skillet until golden brown. Sprinkle with the garlic powder and flour. Cook until very browned. Stir into the broth.

❖ Add the tomatoes and okra. Simmer for 1 hour or until tomatoes are very tender and fall apart.

❖ Add the shrimp, bay leaf, thyme and reserved turkey. Simmer for 3 to 4 hours, stirring occasionally. Remove the bay leaf.

❖ Spoon 1/3 cup rice into serving bowls. Ladle the gumbo over the rice and serve.

❖ May add 1 pound crab meat to the gumbo.

❖ Yield: 8 servings

Approx Per Serving:
Cal 245; Prot 21 g; Carbo 30 g; T Fat 5 g;
18% Calories from Fat; Chol 125 mg;
Fiber 4 g; Sod 599 mg

Linda J. Bove

1 turkey carcass
1 teaspoon salt
1 tablespoon onion flakes
1 onion, chopped
1 tablespoon canola oil
1/8 teaspoon garlic
    powder
2 tablespoons flour
1 (28-ounce) can
    tomatoes
2 (10-ounce) packages
    frozen cut okra
1 pound frozen cooked
    shrimp
1 bay leaf
1/8 teaspoon thyme
2 2/3 cups cooked rice

Zucchini and Pasta Soup with Pistou

Prue Rosenthal

1 cup cubed potatoes
1 teaspoon salt
1 teaspoon pepper
8 cups water
1 onion, chopped
2 large leeks, chopped
2 large carrots, chopped
1 tablespoon margarine
1 tablespoon olive oil
1/4 cup torn spinach
8 ounces green beans
8 ounces tomatoes, chopped
8 ounces zucchini, sliced
2 cups cooked garbanzo beans
1/2 cup uncooked macaroni
1 cup Pistou (page 27)

Cook the potatoes with salt and pepper in water in a saucepan for 30 minutes.

❖ Sauté the onion, leeks and carrots in the margarine and olive oil in a skillet until tender. Add to the potatoes.

❖ Add the spinach, green beans, tomatoes, zucchini, garbanzo beans and macaroni to the potatoes. Cook for 20 minutes. Stir half of the Pistou into the soup.

❖ Ladle the soup into serving bowls. Top each serving with a spoonful of the remaining Pistou or serve separately.

❖ Yield: 6 servings

Approx Per Serving:
Cal 364; Prot 12 g; Carbo 45 g; T Fat 17 g; 40% Calories from Fat; Chol 4 mg; Fiber 9 g; Sod 517 mg

Process the garlic and basil in a food processor until basil is finely chopped.

❖ Add the olive oil and the Parmesan cheese. Process until thickened, but not puréed.

❖ Serve as a garnish for soups, or spread over toasted Italian bread and grill until the Parmesan cheese is melted.

❖ Store in an airtight container in the refrigerator or freezer.

❖ Yield: 8 (1-ounce) servings

Approx Per Serving:
Cal 82; Prot 2 g; Carbo 1 g; T Fat 8 g;
87% Calories from Fat; Chol 3 mg;
Fiber <1 g; Sod 78 mg

Prue Rosenthal

3 cloves of garlic
1 cup fresh basil
$^1/_4$ cup olive oil
$^1/_3$ cup grated Parmesan
　　cheese

27

Appetizers & Soups

Zucchini and Potato Soup

Cecilia Trudeau

2 to 3 medium zucchini,
  sliced
2 to 3 medium potatoes,
  peeled, sliced
2 small onions, sliced
1 quart vegetable or
  chicken broth
1 clove of garlic, minced
1/2 teaspoon salt
1/8 teaspoon pepper
3/4 cup yogurt
Dillweed or curry powder
  to taste

Combine the zucchini, potatoes, onions, broth, garlic, salt and pepper in a large saucepan. Simmer for 30 to 40 minutes or until potatoes are tender.

❖ Pour into a food processor container. Process until puréed.

❖ Ladle into serving bowls. Top with yogurt and dillweed. May serve hot or cold.

❖ Yield: 6 servings

Approx Per Serving:
Cal 93; Prot 3 g; Carbo 17 g; T Fat 2 g;
18% Calories from Fat; Chol 4 mg;
Fiber 2 g; Sod 874 mg

28

Salads

C. S. Mott Children's Hospital

Nurses play a vital part in
Mott's tradition of caring.

Apricot Gelatin Salad

Combine the gelatin, sugar and water in a saucepan. Bring to a boil. Remove from heat and set aside to cool slightly.

❖ Beat the cream cheese and baby food apricots in a bowl. Stir in the pineapple. Fold into the gelatin mixture.

❖ Whip the evaporated milk in a large mixer bowl until thick. Fold in the gelatin mixture and the pecans. Pour into a 9x13-inch glass dish.

❖ Chill for several hours or until firm.

❖ Yield: 15 servings

Approx Per Serving:
Cal 247; Prot 4 g; Carbo 29 g; T Fat 14 g; 49% Calories from Fat; Chol 19 mg; Fiber 1 g; Sod 85 mg

JoAnn Graham

1 (6-ounce) package apricot gelatin
$^2/_3$ cup sugar
$^2/_3$ cup water
8 ounces cream cheese, softened
1 (8-ounce) jar baby food apricots
1 (15-ounce) can pineapple tidbits, drained
1 (5-ounce) can evaporated milk, chilled
1$^1/_2$ cups chopped pecans

31

Salads

Salads

Asparagus in Vinaigrette Sauce

Bring a large pan of lightly salted water to a boil. Add the asparagus. Cook for 3 to 5 minutes. Drain and plunge into ice water to cool. Drain and chill, covered, until serving time.

❖ Beat the egg yolks in a bowl. Add the oil slowly, whisking until thick and creamy. Add the sour cream, tarragon, mustard and tarragon vinegar, whisking until well mixed. Chill until serving time.

❖ Mound the asparagus on a serving platter. Drizzle with the vinaigrette.

❖ Yield: 6 servings

Approx Per Serving:
Cal 414; Prot 7 g; Carbo 11 g; T Fat 40 g; 84% Calories from Fat; Chol 74 mg; Fiber 4 g; Sod 79 mg

Francis Grant

Salt to taste
3 pounds very thin or
    very small asparagus,
    trimmed
2 egg yolks
1 cup vegetable oil
3 tablespoons sour cream
3 tablespoons chopped
    fresh tarragon
1 tablespoon Dijon
    mustard
1 tablespoon tarragon
    vinegar or white wine
    vinegar

33

Salads

Dorthee's Cabbage Salad

Rosanne Whitehouse

1 medium cabbage,
  shredded
1 green bell pepper,
  chopped
1 onion, chopped
3/4 cup sugar
1 teaspoon prepared
  mustard
1 teaspoon celery seeds
1 teaspoon salt
1 teaspoon sugar
3/4 cup cider vinegar
1/2 cup vegetable oil

Combine the cabbage, green pepper and onion in a large bowl. Sprinkle with 3/4 cup sugar and let stand at room temperature, stirring occasionally.

❖ Combine the mustard, celery seeds, salt, 1 teaspoon sugar, vinegar and oil in a small saucepan. Bring to a boil; remove from the heat.

❖ Pour over the cabbage mixture, stirring to coat. Let stand, covered, at room temperature for 4 hours. Chill in the refrigerator until serving time.

❖ Yield: 10 servings

Approx Per Serving:
Cal 188; Prot 2 g; Carbo 23 g; T Fat 11 g;
51% Calories from Fat; Chol 0 mg;
Fiber 2 g; Sod 237 mg

Spread the almonds and sesame seeds on a baking sheet. Bake at 300 degrees until lightly toasted, stirring every 10 minutes; set aside.

❖ Combine the cabbage and green onions in a large salad bowl. Break up the noodles, reserving the flavor packet. Stir the noodles into the cabbage mixture.

❖ Combine the reserved flavor packet, vinegar, sugar, salt and pepper in a small bowl. Add the oil slowly, whisking briskly to mix. Pour over the cabbage mixture just before serving, tossing to coat.

❖ Yield: 10 servings

Approx Per Serving:
Cal 219; Prot 4 g; Carbo 14 g; T Fat 18 g; 70% Calories from Fat; Chol 0 mg; Fiber 2 g; Sod 66 mg

Marilyn Hawkins

1/2 cup slivered almonds
3 tablespoons sesame seeds
1/2 head cabbage, shredded
4 green onions, chopped
1 (3-ounce) package chicken-flavored ramen noodles
3 tablespoons white vinegar
3 tablespoons sugar
1/8 teaspoon salt
1/8 teaspoon pepper
1/2 cup vegetable oil

35

Salads

Fennel, Arugula and Onion Salad

Nicole Stanbridge

1 cup fresh orange juice
2 tablespoons white wine
  vinegar
1 large shallot, sliced
1/2 bay leaf
1 tablespoon extra-virgin
  olive oil
Salt and pepper to taste
1 large fennel bulb,
  trimmed, sliced
2 (1/2-ounce) packages
  arugula, stems
  removed
1/2 medium red onion,
  very thinly sliced
3 oranges

Combine the orange juice, vinegar, shallot and bay leaf in a small saucepan. Bring to a boil. Cook until reduced by half. Discard the bay leaf.

❖ Pour the mixture into a blender container. Process until puréed. Pour into a small bowl. Add the olive oil slowly, whisking briskly until thickened.

❖ Season with salt and pepper. Chill in the refrigerator.

❖ Combine the fennel, arugula and onion in a salad bowl. Add the orange dressing, tossing to coat. Arrange in the center of individual salad plates.

❖ Remove the peel and white membrane from the oranges and cut into sections. Arrange the sections around the edge of each salad.

❖ Yield: 4 servings

Approx Per Serving:
Cal 155; Prot 3 g; Carbo 30 g; T Fat 4 g;
21% Calories from Fat; Chol 0 mg;
Fiber 6 g; Sod 44 mg

Mix the bread, tomatoes, garlic, green pepper, basil and parsley together in a salad bowl.

❖ Combine the olive oil, vinegar, salt and pepper in a tightly covered container. Shake well until mixed. Pour over the bread mixture and toss to coat.

❖ Chill, covered, for 1 hour or longer before serving. Garnish with kalamata or green olives and crumbled feta cheese.

❖ Yield: 6 servings

Approx Per Serving:
Cal 175; Prot 2 g; Carbo 14 g; T Fat 13 g; 65% Calories from Fat; Chol 0 mg; Fiber 1 g; Sod 299 mg

Sara Hickey

4 cups cubed Italian bread
2 medium tomatoes, cut into bite-sized pieces
2 cloves of garlic, minced
1 medium green bell pepper, cut into bite-sized pieces
1/3 cup snipped basil leaves
2 tablespoons snipped parsley
1/3 cup olive oil
2 tablespoons red wine vinegar
1/2 teaspoon salt
1/8 teaspoon pepper

37

Salads

Vegetable and Pasta Salad

Nancy Lyke

16 ounces mixed spinach,
    tomato and egg pasta
1 cup cauliflowerets
1 cup broccoli florets
3 tomatoes, chopped
1/2 cup sliced black olives
1/4 cup chopped onion
1 (8-ounce) bottle of
    Italian salad dressing
1 cup sliced salami or
    pepperoni
1/2 cup grated Parmesan
    cheese
1 cup shredded
    mozzarella cheese

Cook the pasta using package directions. Drain and set aside to cool.

❖ Cook the cauliflowerets and broccoli florets in water to cover in a saucepan until tender. Drain and set aside to cool.

❖ Combine the pasta, cauliflowerets, broccoli florets, tomatoes, olives and onion in a salad bowl. Pour the dressing over the mixture, tossing to coat. Add the salami, Parmesan cheese and mozzarella cheese, tossing to mix.

❖ Chill, covered, for 8 to 10 hours. Toss well before serving.

❖ Yield: 8 servings

Approx Per Serving:
Cal 490; Prot 18 g; Carbo 49 g; T Fat 26 g;
46% Calories from Fat; Chol 27 mg;
Fiber 3 g; Sod 750 mg

38

Pasta Salad with Two-Tomato Vinaigrette

B ring 3 quarts of salted water to a boil in a large kettle. Add the pasta. Cook until al dente. Drain and rinse under cold water.

❖ Combine the drained pasta with the red pepper, scallions, Parmesan cheese and Two-Tomato Vinaigrette in a large salad bowl. Toss well to coat.

❖ Serve at room temperature, or make ahead and chill, covered, in the refrigerator.

❖ Yield: 4 servings

Approx Per Serving:
Cal 397; Prot 14 g; Carbo 50 g; T Fat 17 g; 37% Calories from Fat; Chol 10 mg; Fiber 3 g; Sod 251 mg

Prue Rosenthal

3 quarts water
Salt to taste
8 ounces ziti or other
　　tubular pasta
1/2 red bell pepper, cut
　　into 1-inch strips
3 scallions, chopped
1/2 cup grated Parmesan
　　cheese
2 cups Two-Tomato
　　Vinaigrette (page 46)

39

Salads

Pepper Salad with Capers

Kathy Brennan

1 large ripe tomato
1 clove of garlic, peeled
5 fresh basil leaves, torn
　　into thirds
15 fresh mint leaves
1/4 cup olive oil
Salt and freshly ground
　　pepper to taste
4 large green or yellow
　　bell peppers, or
　　a combination of
　　the two
2 tablespoons capers in
　　wine vinegar, drained

Cut the tomato into pieces. Pass through a food mill into a glass bowl, using the disc with the smallest holes.

❖ Combine with the garlic, basil and 5 of the mint leaves. Drizzle with the oil; season with the salt and pepper. Mix well with a wooden spoon.

❖ Chill, covered with foil, for 1 hour.

❖ Preheat the oven to 375 degrees. Place a pan filled with 4 cups of water on the lower rack of the oven. Leave in the oven for 5 minutes or until the water begins to steam.

❖ Place the whole peppers on the oven rack above the steaming water. Roast for 40 minutes, turning 3 or 4 times.

❖ Place the peppers in a plastic bag. Let stand for 15 minutes. Plunge into a bowl of cold water. Remove the peels, stems and seeds.

❖ Cut the peppers into thin strips. Arrange on a serving dish. Pour the tomato mixture over the peppers, mixing well. Chill, covered with foil, for 1 hour.

❖ Sprinkle with the remaining mint leaves and capers.

❖ Yield: 6 servings

Approx Per Serving:
Cal 104; Prot 1 g; Carbo 6 g; T Fat 9 g;
76% Calories from Fat; Chol 0 mg;
Fiber 1 g; Sod 109 mg

40

Salads

Combine the onion, sour cream, sugar, vinegar, horseradish, mustard and salt in a small bowl; mix well. Stir in the pecans.

❖ Rinse the spinach and drain well. Tear into bite-sized pieces, removing tough stems.

❖ Place in a salad bowl. Pour in the sour cream mixture just before serving. Toss gently to coat.

❖ Yield: 6 servings

Approx Per Serving:
Cal 165; Prot 4 g; Carbo 16 g; T Fat 11 g;
56% Calories from Fat; Chol 9 mg;
Fiber 3 g; Sod 164 mg

Rosanne Whitehouse

1 small onion, chopped
$^1/_2$ cup sour cream
$^1/_4$ cup sugar
$^1/_3$ cup vinegar
2 tablespoons prepared
    horseradish
$^1/_2$ teaspoon dry mustard
$^1/_4$ teaspoon salt
$^1/_2$ cup sliced pecans
16 ounces fresh spinach

41

Salads

Wild Rice and Chicken Salad

Judy Bliss

1/2 cup mayonnaise-type
    salad dressing
1/3 cup sour cream
1/2 teaspoon salt
1/4 teaspoon crushed
    marjoram leaves
1/8 teaspoon white pepper
3 cups cooked wild rice,
    chilled
2 cups cubed cooked
    chicken
1/2 cup diagonally-sliced
    celery
1/2 cup coarsely chopped
    red bell pepper
1/2 cup sliced fresh
    mushrooms
1/4 cup diagonally-sliced
    green onions
1 small head lettuce
3 tomatoes, cut into
    wedges
1/4 cup toasted slivered
    almonds

Mix the mayonnaise-type salad dressing and sour cream in a small bowl until blended. Stir in the salt, marjoram and white pepper; set aside.

❖ Combine the rice, chicken, celery, red pepper, mushrooms and green onions in a large bowl. Add the salad dressing mixture, tossing gently.

❖ Chill, covered, for 2 to 3 hours to blend flavors.

❖ Place the lettuce leaves on 6 individual salad plates. Spoon an equal amount of the chicken salad mixture over the lettuce. Arrange the tomato wedges around the edge. Sprinkle with the almonds.

❖ Yield: 6 servings

Approx Per Serving:
Cal 337; Prot 20 g; Carbo 30 g; T Fat 16 g;
43% Calories from Fat; Chol 52 mg;
Fiber 4 g; Sod 388 mg

42

Brandy's Tuna Salad Surprise

Flake the tuna into a medium bowl. Stir in the apple, onion, celery, raisins and almonds. Add the salad dressing and mix well.

❖ Serve over lettuce leaves or spread over party bread for mini-sandwiches. May vary the amount of apple, onion, raisins and almonds.

❖ Yield: 6 servings

Approx Per Serving:
Cal 345; Prot 32 g; Carbo 33 g; T Fat 10 g; 26% Calories from Fat; Chol 34 mg; Fiber 4 g; Sod 560 mg

Jim Brandstatter

Color Commentator, Detroit Lions, Michigan Football, Friend of Mott Children's Hospital

4 (6-ounce) cans water-
    packed tuna, drained
1 Red Delicious apple, cut
    into cubes
1 sweet onion, chopped
2 ribs celery, chopped
1 cup raisins
1 (2-ounce) package
    sliced almonds
1/2 cup low-fat
    mayonnaise-type
    salad dressing

43

Salads

Salmon with Asparagus, Peas and Potatoes

Prue Rosenthal

Baked Minted Salmon

1¹/2 pounds salmon fillets
¹/2 teaspoon salt
Freshly ground pepper to
    taste
2 teaspoons lemon juice
Salt and pepper to taste
2 teaspoons finely
    chopped fresh mint

Marinated Asparagus
and Peas

24 asparagus spears
Salt to taste
12 ounces sugar snap
    peas
1¹/2 cups cooked peas
3 tablespoons Lemon
    Vinaigrette (page 46)
Pepper to taste

Baked Minted Salmon

Place the salmon on a baking sheet;
season with ¹/2 teaspoon salt and
freshly ground pepper.

❖ Bake at 350 degrees for 20 minutes or
until salmon flakes easily; cool. Cut into
chunks, discarding skin.

❖ Toss gently with 2 teaspoons lemon
juice, salt and pepper in a bowl. Sprinkle
with mint.

❖ Chill until serving time.

Marinated Asparagus and Peas

❖ Cut the tips from the asparagus. Trim
and peel the stalks. Cut into 1-inch
pieces. Blanch the stalks in boiling salted
water in a saucepan for 2 minutes. Add
the tips. Blanch for 1 minute longer.
Drain and rinse under cold water.

❖ Blanch the sugar snap peas in boiling
salted water in a saucepan for 4 minutes.
Drain well.

❖ Combine the asparagus, sugar snap
peas and cooked peas in a glass bowl.
Toss with 3 tablespoons of the Lemon
Vinaigrette. Season with salt and pepper.
Chill until serving time.

44

Salads

Salmon with Asparagus, Peas and Potatoes

Yogurt Potato Salad

❖ Whisk the mayonnaise, yogurt, lime zest, lime juice, scallions, 3/4 teaspoon salt and pepper to taste in a glass bowl. Add the potatoes, tossing gently to coat. Chill until serving time.

❖ Toss the salad greens with 3 tablespoons Lemon Vinaigrette in a salad bowl.

❖ Serve each item separately, allowing guests to build their own salads.

❖ Yield: 6 servings

Approx Per Serving:
Cal 548; Prot 35 g; Carbo 43 g; T Fat 27 g; 44% Calories from Fat; Chol 85 mg; Fiber 8 g; Sod 704 mg

Yogurt Potato Salad

1/4 cup mayonnaise
5 tablespoons low-fat
    yogurt
3/4 teaspoon lime zest
2 teaspoons lime juice
1 or 2 scallions, chopped
3/4 teaspoon salt
Pepper to taste
1 1/2 pounds small red
    potatoes, cut into
    1/2-inch slices, cooked,
    drained

12 cups mixed salad
    greens
3 tablespoons Lemon
    Vinaigrette (page 46)

45

Salads

Lemon Vinaigrette

Prue Rosenthal

1 teaspoon Dijon mustard
1/4 cup fresh lemon juice
1/2 teaspoon kosher salt
1/2 cup olive oil

Whisk the first 3 ingredients in a bowl until blended. Add the olive oil slowly, whisking until slightly thickened.

❖ Store, tightly covered, in the refrigerator. Bring to room temperature to serve, stirring well.

❖ Yield: 6 (1-ounce) servings

Approx Per Serving:
Cal 163; Prot <1 g; Carbo 1 g; T Fat 18 g; 98% Calories from Fat; Chol 0 mg; Fiber <1 g; Sod 200 mg

Two-Tomato Vinaigrette

Prue Rosenthal

6 plum tomatoes
1 teaspoon olive oil
1 tablespoon minced
    garlic
Salt and pepper to taste
2 tablespoons balsamic
    vinegar
3 tablespoons finely
    chopped oil-pack
    sun-dried tomatoes
3 tablespoons tomato oil

Slice the tomatoes into halves. Arrange cut side up in a greased 8-inch square baking dish. Brush with the olive oil. Sprinkle with the garlic, salt and pepper.

❖ Bake at 450 degrees on the center oven rack for 40 minutes or until the tomatoes are very tender. Chop the tomatoes coarsely. Combine with the vinegar in a small bowl.

❖ Stir the sun-dried tomatoes and the tomato oil into the tomato mixture. Store, covered, in the refrigerator. Bring to room temperature before serving.

❖ Yield: 4 servings

Approx Per Serving:
Cal 125; Prot 1 g; Carbo 5 g; T Fat 12 g; 81% Calories from Fat; Chol 0 mg; Fiber 1 g; Sod 13 mg

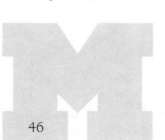

Salads

Main Dishes

Deborah Kingen

Head Chef, Deborah Kingen, of the Michigan Star Clipper Dinner Train.

Heat a sauté pan over medium heat. Add the olive oil, 1/2 teaspoon butter, shrimp, shallots, scallops, salt, pepper and crab meat. Sauté for several minutes. Remove the shrimp mixture and keep warm.

❖ Add the wine to the sauté pan. Cook until deglazed. Add the whipping cream. Cook until reduced by 1/4. Stir in the Dijon mustard and basil. Sauté until of the desired consistency. Set aside and keep warm.

❖ Brush the dough lightly with the melted butter and stack the sheets together. Place the shrimp mixture in the center of the dough. Gather into a bundle and tie with the scallion, trimming excess dough if needed. Place on an ovenproof fish plate or baking sheet. Bake at 350 degrees for 3 minutes.

❖ Place the phyllo pouch on a 5-inch plate. Spoon the sauce to the side. Arrange the red pepper strips over the sauce in a V.

❖ Yield: 1 serving

Approx Per Serving:
Cal 837; Prot 30 g; Carbo 41 g; T Fat 60 g;
64% Calories from Fat; Chol 227 mg;
Fiber 2 g; Sod 1122 mg

Deborah Kingen

1 teaspoon olive oil
1/2 teaspoon butter
2 shrimp, peeled, deveined
1 teaspoon chopped shallots
3 scallops
Salt and pepper to taste
1/4 cup crab meat
2 tablespoons white wine, or to taste
1/4 cup whipping cream
1/8 teaspoon Dijon mustard, or to taste
Chopped fresh basil to taste
3 sheets phyllo dough
2 tablespoons melted butter
1 green scallion
2 thin strips red bell pepper

49

Main Dishes

Main Dishes

Stuffed Fillets of Sole

Sauté the crab meat in 1 tablespoon butter in a skillet. Add the shallots. Sauté for 1 minute.

❖ Rinse the fish with cold water and pat dry. Sprinkle with salt and pepper. Arrange half the fillets in a single layer in a buttered 9x13-inch baking pan. Top with the crab meat mixture. Add the remaining fillets. Sprinkle with the lemon juice. Dot with 1 tablespoon butter. Top with the bread crumbs.

❖ Bake at 450 degrees until the fish flakes easily.

❖ Serve with lemon wedges.

❖ Yield: 4 servings

Approx Per Serving:
Cal 397; Prot 67 g; Carbo 5 g; T Fat 10 g; 25% Calories from Fat; Chol 227 mg; Fiber <1 g; Sod 483 mg

Diane Chambre

8 ounces crab meat
1 tablespoon butter
1/4 cup chopped shallots
8 (4- to 5-ounce) sole fillets
Salt and pepper to taste
1/4 cup lemon juice
1 tablespoon butter
2 tablespoons dry bread crumbs

51

Main Dishes

Endive Boats with Smoked Salmon Stuffing

George Tattersfield

6 ounces smoked salmon,
    coarsely chopped
2 tablespoons extra-virgin
    olive oil
1 tablespoon fresh lemon
    juice
2 tablespoons snipped
    fresh chives
Salt and freshly ground
    pepper to taste
4 large Belgian endives
2 tablespoons salmon roe

Combine the smoked salmon, olive oil, lemon juice, chives, salt and pepper in a bowl and mix well. Marinate, covered, in the refrigerator for 1 hour.

❖ Remove the outer leaves of the endives; discard or reserve for another use. Separate from each endive 6 to 8 tender leaves that are large enough for stuffing. Chill thoroughly.

❖ Stir the salmon roe gently into the smoked salmon mixture. Spoon into the endive leaves, or "boats." Arrange on a platter and serve immediately.

❖ Yield: 8 servings

Approx Per Serving:
Cal 68; Prot 5 g; Carbo 1 g; T Fat 5 g;
67% Calories from Fat; Chol 29 mg;
Fiber <1 g; Sod 227 mg

Salmon Burgers

Combine the salmon, bread crumbs, Dijon mustard, onion, lemon juice, garlic, salt and pepper in a bowl and mix well. Shape into four 1/2x4-inch patties; the patties will be fragile. Place on a plate. Chill until needed.

❖ Heat the grill until the coals glow red with a white ash around the edge. Place the patties 2 inches apart on the grill rack. Grill for 2 minutes per side or just until cooked through, turning once.

❖ Serve on the buns and spread with mayonnaise or tartar sauce.

❖ Yield: 4 servings

Approx Per Serving:
Cal 395; Prot 29 g; Carbo 26 g; T Fat 18 g; 43% Calories from Fat; Chol 83 mg; Fiber 1 g; Sod 744 mg

Juliette Jonna

1 (1-pound) boneless skinless salmon fillet, finely chopped
2 tablespoons bread crumbs
1 tablespoon Dijon mustard
1 tablespoon minced onion
2 teaspoons lemon juice
1/2 teaspoon minced or pressed garlic
1/2 teaspoon salt, or to taste
1/2 teaspoon freshly ground pepper
4 hamburger buns
1 1/2 to 2 tablespoons mayonnaise or tartar sauce

53

Main Dishes

Scallops Sauté

Rhonda Schoville

2 tablespoons reduced-
    calorie margarine
1 pound fresh sugar snap
    peas
2¹/₂ cups diagonally
    sliced celery
1 pound fresh sea scallops
¹/₄ cup chablis or other
    dry white wine
3 tablespoons lemon juice
¹/₂ teaspoon dried whole
    dillweed
¹/₂ teaspoon freshly
    ground pepper
2 tablespoons chopped
    fresh parsley

Melt the margarine in a large nonstick skillet sprayed with nonstick cooking spray over medium-high heat. Add the peas and celery. Sauté for 3 to 4 minutes or until tender-crisp. Remove the vegetables with a slotted spoon.

❖ Add the scallops, wine, lemon juice, dillweed and pepper to the skillet. Bring to a boil; reduce the heat. Simmer, covered, for 5 to 6 minutes or until the scallops are opaque. Add the cooked vegetables. Cook just until heated through.

❖ Sprinkle with the parsley. Serve with a slotted spoon.

❖ Yield: 4 servings

Approx Per Serving:
Cal 202; Prot 19 g; Carbo 15 g; T Fat 7 g;
30% Calories from Fat; Chol 29 mg;
Fiber 4 g; Sod 274 mg

54

Main Dishes

Shrimp Elegante

Melt 3 tablespoons butter in a skillet. Add the shrimp and mushrooms. Cook over medium heat until the mushrooms are tender and the shrimp turn pink, stirring frequently. Remove and keep warm.

❖ Melt 1/4 cup butter in the skillet. Blend in the flour, mustard and cayenne. Stir in the cream. Cook until thickened, stirring frequently.

❖ Add the shrimp mixture. Cook for 2 to 3 minutes or until heated through. Stir in the sherry and cheese.

❖ Serve over the rice.

❖ Yield: 8 servings

Approx Per Serving:
Cal 576; Prot 24 g; Carbo 49 g; T Fat 31 g; 49% Calories from Fat; Chol 245 mg; Fiber 1 g; Sod 355 mg

Katherine Prasol

3 tablespoons butter
1 (27-ounce) package frozen shelled shrimp, thawed
4 ounces fresh mushrooms
1/4 cup butter
1/4 cup flour
1/4 teaspoon dry mustard
1/8 teaspoon cayenne, or to taste
2 cups light cream
3 tablespoons sherry
1/4 cup grated Parmesan cheese
4 to 6 cups cooked white rice

Main Dishes

Shrimp Newburg

Walter Szepelak

12 ounces shrimp
3 tablespoons butter
$1/2$ cup sherry
$1/8$ teaspoon paprika
$1/8$ teaspoon dry mustard
1 can cream of mushroom
    soup
$1/3$ cup light cream
Salt and pepper to taste
2 to 3 cups cooked white
    rice

Sauté the shrimp in the butter in a skillet. Add the sherry. Simmer gently until the liquid is reduced by $1/2$.

❖ Add the paprika, mustard, soup and cream and mix well. Simmer for 5 minutes.

❖ Season with salt and pepper. Serve over the rice.

❖ Yield: 4 servings

Approx Per Serving:
Cal 501; Prot 20 g; Carbo 50 g; T Fat 22 g; 39% Calories from Fat; Chol 179 mg; Fiber 1 g; Sod 869 mg

Portland Maine Baked Stuffed Shrimp

Arrange the shrimp in a single layer on a nonstick baking sheet.

❖ Melt 3/4 cup butter in a saucepan. Remove from the heat. Add the cracker crumbs and mix well. Stir in the lobster.

❖ Spread 1 1/2 tablespoons of the stuffing over each shrimp. Sprinkle with the melted butter.

❖ Bake at 400 degrees for 18 to 20 minutes or until the shrimp turn pink.

❖ Yield: 8 servings

Approx Per Serving:
Cal 302; Prot 11 g; Carbo 16 g; T Fat 22 g;
64% Calories from Fat; Chol 98 mg;
Fiber 1 g; Sod 611 mg

Ellen Gaucher

16 jumbo shrimp, peeled, butterflied
3/4 cup butter
1 1/2 sleeves saltines, finely crushed
1 (7-ounce) can lobster body meat, or 7 ounces fresh
2 to 3 teaspoons melted butter

57

Almond Boneless Chicken

Diane Shember

Crispy Chicken

2 whole boneless skinless
    chicken breasts, split
    into halves
$1/2$ teaspoon salt
1 tablespoon dry sherry
3 tablespoons cornstarch
3 tablespoons flour
$1/2$ teaspoon baking
    powder
1 egg, beaten
1 tablespoon water
Vegetable oil for frying

Crispy Chicken

Rinse the chicken and pat dry. Sprinkle the chicken with the salt and sherry. Let stand for 15 minutes.

❖ Beat 3 tablespoons cornstarch, flour, baking powder, egg and 1 tablespoon water in a bowl until smooth.

❖ Coat the chicken with the cornstarch mixture.

❖ Pour enough oil into a large skillet or wok to measure $1/2$ inch.

❖ Heat the oil to 375 degrees.

❖ Add the chicken. Cook for 5 to 7 minutes or until golden brown, turning once.

❖ Drain on paper towels. Cut into diagonal strips.

58

Main Dishes

Mushroom Sauce

❖ Combine 1/4 cup cornstarch and 3 tablespoons water in a small saucepan over medium heat, stirring until smooth.

❖ Add the chicken broth and mushrooms gradually, stirring after each addition.

❖ Add the chicken fat, soy sauce and instant bouillon. Bring to a boil, stirring constantly.

❖ Boil for 1 minute.

❖ Arrange the chicken strips over the lettuce. Sprinkle with the almonds and green onion.

❖ Pour the mushroom sauce over the chicken.

❖ Serve immediately with rice.

❖ Yield: 6 servings

Approx Per Serving:
Cal 294; Prot 24 g; Carbo 16 g; T Fat 14 g;
44% Calories from Fat; Chol 90 mg;
Fiber 1 g; Sod 1568 mg
Nutritional information does not include oil for frying.

Mushroom Sauce

1/4 cup cornstarch
3 tablespoons water
3 cups chicken broth
1 1/2 cups chopped mushrooms
3 tablespoons chicken fat or butter
2 tablespoons soy sauce
1 tablespoon instant chicken bouillon

1 cup shredded lettuce
1/3 cup toasted slivered almonds
1 green onion, finely chopped

59

Main Dishes

Cashew Chicken with Lime Dipping Sauce

Marge Tattersfield

2 pounds boneless
    skinless chicken
    breasts
1/4 cup dry sherry
1/4 cup soy sauce
1 tablespoon sesame oil
2 tablespoons fresh lime
    juice
Finely grated zest of 1
    lime
2 cloves of garlic, minced
1 1/2 tablespoons minced
    fresh ginger
1 1/2 cups lightly toasted
    cashews
1/2 cup sesame seeds
1/2 cup cornstarch
1 (16-ounce) jar lime
    marmalade
1 (5-ounce) jar prepared
    white horseradish
3 tablespoons chopped
    cilantro

Rinse the chicken and pat dry. Cut into 1-inch cubes. Whisk the sherry, soy sauce, sesame oil and lime juice in a large bowl. Stir in the lime zest, garlic and ginger. Add the chicken, tossing to coat. Marinate in the refrigerator for 2 hours or longer.

❖ Combine the cashews, sesame seeds and cornstarch in a food processor container. Process until crumbly. Pour into a shallow dish or pie plate.

❖ Remove the chicken from the marinade, reserving the remaining marinade. Dredge the chicken evenly with the cashew mixture. Spread the chicken on a lightly oiled baking sheet.

❖ Bake at 375 degrees for 10 minutes or just until the chicken is cooked through, drizzling occasionally with the reserved marinade.

❖ Heat the marmalade in a saucepan over medium-low heat just until melted. Remove from the heat. Stir in the horseradish and cilantro. Pour into a small bowl.

❖ Spear each chicken cube with a wooden pick. Arrange on a serving platter. Serve with the sauce.

❖ Yield: 30 servings

Approx Per Serving:
Cal 146; Prot 9 g; Carbo 15 g; T Fat 6 g;
35% Calories from Fat; Chol 19 mg;
Fiber 1 g; Sod 169 mg

60

Main Dishes

Chicken Breasts in White Wine

Rinse the chicken and pat dry. Sprinkle the chicken with the salt, pepper and paprika. Coat with the flour.

❖ Melt half the butter in a large skillet. Add the chicken. Cook until browned, turning once. Remove the chicken and set aside.

❖ Add the remaining 1/4 cup butter to the skillet. Add the mushrooms, green onions, celery and garlic. Cook until the garlic is tender and golden brown.

❖ Return the chicken to the skillet. Add the wine. Simmer, covered, for 45 minutes or until the chicken is tender and cooked through.

❖ Serve with a tossed green salad.

❖ May serve over noodles or rice.

❖ Yield: 4 servings

Approx Per Serving:
Cal 471; Prot 36 g; Carbo 11 g; T Fat 27 g; 52% Calories from Fat; Chol 154 mg; Fiber 1 g; Sod 878 mg

Trudy Widner

4 large chicken breasts, deboned, split into halves
1 teaspoon salt
1/8 teaspoon pepper
1/8 teaspoon paprika
1/3 cup flour
1/2 cup butter
1 cup sliced fresh mushrooms
1/2 cup chopped green onions
1 cup chopped celery
1 small clove of garlic, thinly sliced
1 cup white wine

Chicken Oriental

Kathy Mount

6 chicken breasts,
    deboned
1/4 cup butter
1/2 cup dry sherry
1/2 cup water
Salt and pepper to taste
1 (10-ounce) package
    frozen Japanese
    vegetables
1 (10-ounce) package
    frozen Italian
    vegetables
1 cup milk
2 tablespoons cornstarch
4 to 6 cups cooked
    wild rice

*Kathy Mount of Plymouth and her very
special dog Bambi entertain the children of
Mott Hospital at least once a month. Kathy
has raised more than $60,000 for Mott
Hospital over the past three years.*

Rinse the chicken and pat dry. Split
the chicken into halves; cut into bite-
size pieces.

❖ Melt the butter in a wok. Add a few
pieces of chicken at a time. Cook until
browned. Add the sherry and water.
Season with the salt and pepper. Cook,
covered, at 300 degrees for 20 minutes.

❖ Stir in the frozen vegetables. Blend the
milk and cornstarch in a bowl. Stir into
the chicken mixture. Cook, covered, over
low heat for 45 minutes or until the
vegetables are tender and the chicken
is cooked through, stirring occasionally
if needed.

❖ Serve over the rice.

❖ Yield: 8 servings

Approx Per Serving:
Cal 345; Prot 28 g; Carbo 35 g; T Fat 9 g;
25% Calories from Fat; Chol 75 mg;
Fiber 4 g; Sod 146 mg

Rinse the chicken and pat dry. Heat a nonstick Dutch oven sprayed with nonstick cooking spray over medium heat. Add the onion, celery and garlic. Cook for 3 to 5 minutes or until tender, stirring frequently.

❖ Add the chicken, undrained tomatoes, rice, instant bouillon, bay leaf and pepper. Bring to a boil; reduce the heat to low. Simmer, covered, for 30 minutes, stirring frequently.

❖ Add the peas. Simmer, covered, for 10 minutes, stirring frequently. Remove the bay leaf.

❖ May add chicken broth or water during simmering if needed. May omit the peas.

❖ Yield: 6 servings

Approx Per Serving:
Cal 259; Prot 16 g; Carbo 38 g; T Fat 5 g;
17% Calories from Fat; Chol 36 mg;
Fiber 4 g; Sod 605 mg

Frances L. Rupp

1 pound skinless chicken
    thighs, deboned
1 cup chopped onion
1/2 cup chopped celery
2 cloves of garlic, finely
    chopped
1 (16-ounce) can chopped
    tomatoes, or
    2 (14-ounce) cans
    Italian tomatoes
1 cup long grain rice
1 teaspoon instant
    chicken bouillon, or
    2 chicken bouillon
    cubes
1 bay leaf
1/4 teaspoon ground
    pepper
1 (10-ounce) package
    frozen green peas

63

Main Dishes

Coq au Vin Gaucher

Steve Gaucher

4 ounces Canadian bacon,
  chopped
1 onion, cut into quarters
8 carrots, cut into quarters
2 tablespoons butter
1 (5-pound) chicken, cut
  into serving pieces
2 tablespoons flour
Salt and pepper to taste
1/4 cup brandy
1 (750-milliliter) bottle
  French red burgundy
1 clove of garlic, crushed
1 bouquet garni
1 sugar cube
2 cups dried porcini
  mushrooms
1 cup warm water
5 tablespoons butter,
  softened
5 tablespoons flour

Sauté the bacon, onion and carrots in 2 tablespoons butter in a large heavy saucepan over medium heat until the onion is tender but not browned.

❖ Rinse the chicken; pat dry. Coat with 2 tablespoons flour; season with salt and pepper. Add to the saucepan. Cook over medium-high heat until brown.

❖ Heat the brandy in a small saucepan. Light it with a match and pour over the chicken. Add the wine when the flames subside, stirring to deglaze the pan.

❖ Add the next 3 ingredients. Bring to a boil; reduce heat. Simmer for 30 minutes or until the chicken is tender.

❖ Soak the mushrooms in the warm water for 20 minutes or until softened; drain on paper towels. Chop into bite-size pieces. Add to the chicken mixture. Simmer for 30 minutes longer, stirring occasionally; remove from the heat.

❖ Remove the chicken with a slotted spoon and set aside. Skim the fat from the liquid and discard the bouquet garni.

❖ Prepare a beurre manié by kneading the remaining butter with the remaining flour. Shape into small balls and drop into the liquid, stirring constantly until smooth. Bring to a boil. Cook until thickened, stirring constantly; reduce the heat to low. Add the chicken. Heat for 5 minutes before serving.

❖ Yield: 8 servings

Approx Per Serving:
Cal 584; Prot 48 g; Carbo 30 g; T Fat 22 g;
34% Calories from Fat; Chol 161 mg;
Fiber 5g; Sod 476 mg

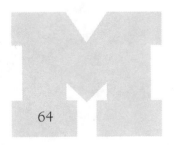

Main Dishes

Rinse the chicken and pat dry. Rub inside and out with $1/2$ clove of garlic, salt, pepper and herbes de Provence. Place a small amount of the butter in the cavity. Place the chicken on a rack in a roaster pan. Rub with a small amount of the remaining butter.

❖ Roast at 450 degrees for 15 minutes. Turn the chicken and rub with a small amount of the remaining butter. Roast for 15 minutes longer. Reduce the oven temperature to 375 degrees. Roast for 30 to 40 minutes or until the chicken is tender and cooked through and the juices run clear, basting occasionally.

❖ Combine the giblets, onion, carrot, bouquet garni and lemon peel with water to cover in a saucepan. Simmer over low heat while the chicken is roasting.

❖ Remove the chicken from the roaster and keep warm. Strain the fat from the pan drippings. Bring the pan drippings to a boil in the roaster. Strain $1/4$ cup of the giblet stock into the roaster. Bring to a rapid boil. Blend the flour and remaining butter in a bowl. Add to the pan drippings, stirring until smooth. Season to taste. Return to a boil. Simmer for 1 minute. Strain into a gravy boat. Serve with the chicken.

❖ Yield: 8 servings

Approx Per Serving:
Cal 315; Prot 31 g; Carbo 3 g; T Fat 19 g;
56% Calories from Fat; Chol 125 mg;
Fiber 1 g; Sod 212 mg

Kathy Gaucher

1 large roasting chicken
   with giblets
$1/2$ clove of garlic
Salt and freshly ground
   pepper to taste
1 teaspoon herbes de
   Provence
$1/2$ cup butter
1 onion, cut into quarters
1 carrot, cut into quarters
1 bouquet garni
Strips of lemon peel
1 teaspoon flour

65

Main Dishes

Ground Turkey Burgers

Nancy Lyke

2 pounds freshly ground
   turkey
1/2 cup chopped onion
2 egg whites
3/4 cup bread crumbs
Salt and pepper to taste
Parsley flakes to taste
8 whole wheat hamburger
   buns

Combine the turkey, onion, egg whites, bread crumbs, salt, pepper and parsley in a bowl and mix well. Shape into patties.

❖ Cook in a nonstick skillet sprayed with nonstick cooking spray until the turkey is no longer pink.

❖ Serve on the buns. Serve with K.C. Masterpiece B-B-Q Sauce.

❖ May prepare patties ahead and freeze until needed.

❖ Yield: 8 servings

Approx Per Serving:
Cal 364; Prot 30 g; Carbo 28 g; T Fat 15 g;
36% Calories from Fat; Chol 87 mg;
Fiber 2 g; Sod 392 mg

Lamb Chops with Tequila and Honey

Cindy, the Director of Customer Relations for Northwest Airlines, has worked on several fund raisers for our hospital. She can always be counted on to support Mott.

Combine the olive oil, juice of 1 lime, cumin, cayenne and chili powder in a bowl. Add the lamb chops. Marinate in the refrigerator for 4 hours or longer.

❖ Combine the veal stock and remaining lime juice in a saucepan. Cook for 10 minutes or until the mixture begins to reduce and thicken. Add the honey. Simmer for 5 minutes. Add the tequila. Simmer for 1 minute. Stir in the butter at serving time. Season with salt and pepper.

❖ Remove the lamb chops from the marinade. Grill or broil to the desired degree of doneness.

❖ Spoon the tequila sauce over the lamb chops. Garnish with julienned lime peel.

❖ May substitute loin or shoulder chops for the rib chops.

❖ Yield: 4 servings

Approx Per Serving:
Cal 747; Prot 43 g; Carbo 19 g; T Fat 52 g; 63% Calories from Fat; Chol 162 mg; Fiber <1 g; Sod 625 mg

Cindy Scheer

1/2 cup olive oil
Juice of 1 1/2 limes
1/8 teaspoon ground cumin, or to taste
1/8 teaspoon cayenne, or to taste
1/8 teaspoon chili powder, or to taste
12 rib lamp chops
2 cups reduced veal stock or lamb stock
1/4 cup honey
1/4 cup tequila
1/4 cup butter
Salt and pepper to taste

Main Dishes

Rack of Lamb

Jean Henrickson

2 tablespoons minced
   garlic
1/2 cup olive oil
2 tablespoons fresh
   rosemary
1/2 cup Dijon mustard
2 teaspoons pepper
1/4 cup soy sauce
1/8 teaspoon salt
4 racks of lamb
1/2 cup Sungiovese wine
1/2 cup sherry
1 tablespoon roasted
   garlic
1 tablespoon fresh
   rosemary
2 tablespoons butter
5 cups beef stock
1/2 cup minced shallots
1 tablespoon lemon juice
1/2 teaspoon pepper
Salt to taste

Combine the minced garlic, olive oil, 2 tablespoons rosemary, Dijon mustard, 2 teaspoons pepper, soy sauce and 1/8 teaspoon salt in a large sealable plastic bag. Add the lamb. Marinate in the refrigerator for 8 hours.

❖ Combine the wine and sherry in a saucepan. Cook until reduced to 1/2 cup. Add the roasted garlic, 1 tablespoon rosemary, butter, beef stock, shallots, lemon juice, 1/2 teaspoon pepper and salt to taste and mix well. Simmer for 30 minutes.

❖ Grill over hot coals for 3 to 4 minutes on each side or to desired degree of doneness.

❖ Serve the sauce over the lamb.

❖ Yield: 8 servings

Approx Per Serving:
Cal 1163; Prot 110 g; Carbo 5 g; T Fat 73 g; 58% Calories from Fat; Chol 367 mg; Fiber <1 g; Sod 1799 mg

Spicy Pork Tenderloin

Combine the chili powder, salt, ginger, thyme and pepper in a bowl and mix well. Rub over the tenderloins. Marinate, covered, in the refrigerator for 2 to 4 hours.

❖ Remove the tenderloins from the marinade. Grill over hot coals for 15 minutes per side or until the juices run clear; the spices will appear burned.

❖ Cut into 1-inch slices.

❖ Yield: 8 servings

Approx Per Serving:
Cal 124; Prot 20 g; Carbo 2 g; T Fat 4 g;
29% Calories from Fat; Chol 56 mg;
Fiber 1 g; Sod 334 mg

Maggie Brownridge

1 to 3 tablespoons chili
   powder
1 teaspoon salt
1/4 teaspoon ground
   ginger
1/4 teaspoon ground
   thyme
1/4 teaspoon pepper
2 (1-pound) pork
   tenderloins

69

Main Dishes

Venison-Stuffed Cabbage

Michael Boyd

Ann Arbor Businessman

3 pounds ground venison
1 envelope onion soup
    mix
1 teaspoon garlic salt
1 egg
1/2 cup milk
1 cup uncooked white rice
1/2 cup steak sauce
1/4 cup catsup
1 large head cabbage
1 (15-ounce) can tomato
    sauce

Mike organizes a golf tournament each year to benefit the children at Mott Hospital.

Combine the venison, soup mix, garlic salt, egg, milk, rice, steak sauce and catsup in a bowl and mix well.

❖ Boil the cabbage in water to cover in a saucepan for 15 minutes. Let cool. Remove the cabbage leaves and fill 1/3 full with the venison mixture. Roll up and secure with wooden picks.

❖ Place the cabbage rolls in a 9x12-inch baking pan. Pour the tomato sauce over the rolls.

❖ Bake, covered, at 325 degrees for 2 hours.

❖ May substitute ground beef for the venison.

❖ Yield: 10 servings

Approx Per Serving:
Cal 301; Prot 36 g; Carbo 29 g; T Fat 5 g;
14% Calories from Fat; Chol 137 mg;
Fiber 3 g; Sod 869 mg

70

Grand Marnier Veal Shanks

Steve Gaucher

Dredge the veal in the flour. Brown in 3 tablespoons of the oil in a large casserole. Remove the veal to a plate and drain the casserole.

❖ Add the remaining 2 tablespoons oil to the casserole. Add the onion, celery, carrot and 3 cloves of garlic. Cook over moderate heat until the onion is golden brown, stirring constantly. Add the wine and 1/4 cup Grand Marnier. Boil for 2 minutes. Add the beef broth, tomatoes, thyme, basil, rosemary, bay leaf and orange peel strips. Bring to a simmer.

❖ Add the veal to the mixture in the casserole. Cover and place in a preheated 350-degree oven. Bake for 1 1/2 to 2 hours or to desired degree of doneness. Remove to a plate. Skim the cooking liquid.

❖ Mix the cornstarch with 2 tablespoons Grand Marnier in a small bowl. Bring the cooking liquid to a boil. Stir in the cornstarch mixture. Simmer for 2 to 3 minutes or until thickened, stirring constantly. Stir into the beef broth mixture. Heat until warmed through.

❖ Mix the grated orange peel, lemon peel, parsley and 1 teaspoon garlic in a bowl.

❖ Spoon the sauce over the veal. Top with the parsley mixture.

❖ Yield: 4 servings

Approx Per Serving:
Cal 696; Prot 60 g; Carbo 29 g; T Fat 27 g; 36% Calories from Fat; Chol 207 mg; Fiber 4 g; Sod 466 mg

8 (2-inch) veal shanks
1/4 to 1/2 cup flour
5 tablespoons vegetable oil
1 cup minced onion
1/2 cup minced celery
1/2 cup minced carrot
3 cloves of garlic, minced
1 cup dry white wine
1/4 cup Grand Marnier
1 1/2 cups beef broth
1 1/2 cups crushed tomatoes
1/2 teaspoon dried thyme
1/2 teaspoon basil
1/2 teaspoon rosemary
1 bay leaf
2 (3-inch) strips of orange peel
2 tablespoons cornstarch
2 tablespoons Grand Marnier
1 tablespoon grated orange peel
1 tablespoon grated lemon peel
1/4 cup parsley
1 teaspoon minced garlic

71

Main Dishes

Escapole de Veau à la Moutarde

*Rod and Sandra
Campbell*

8 veal scaloppine, about
    12 ounces
1/3 cup flour
Salt and freshly ground
    pepper to taste
1/4 cup butter
2 tablespoons finely
    minced shallots
1/4 cup dry white wine
1/2 cup whipping cream
1 tablespoon Dijon
    mustard

*Rod and Sandra Campbell have demon-
strated their concern for the health care of
the children of Michigan by their generous
support of Mott Children's Hospital.*

P ound the veal very thin. Dredge
with a mixture of the flour, salt
and pepper.

❖ Heat the butter in a skillet. Add the
veal. Cook for 2 minutes per side or until
golden brown. Remove and keep warm.

❖ Add the shallots to the skillet. Cook
briefly. Add the wine. Cook until most
of the wine has evaporated, stirring
constantly.

❖ Add the whipping cream. Bring to a
boil; remove from the heat. Stir in the
mustard.

❖ Serve the sauce over the veal.

❖ Yield: 4 servings

Approx Per Serving:
Cal 1382; Prot 19 g; Carbo 19 g; T Fat 32 g;
21% Calories from Fat; Chol 131 mg;
Fiber <1 g; Sod 332 mg

Main Dishes

Trim the fat from the brisket. Place the brisket in a large flat roaster. Season with the salt and pepper. Cover with the onions, celery and chili sauce. Pour in the water.

❖ Roast, uncovered, at 325 degrees for 1¹/₂ hours, basting every 15 minutes. Roast, covered, for 1 hour. Add the beer. Roast for 1 to 1¹/₂ hours or to desired degree of doneness.

❖ Combine the onions, celery and pan drippings in a food processor container. Process until puréed.

❖ Cut the beef into slices. Serve with the sauce.

❖ Yield: 10 servings

Approx Per Serving:
Cal 376; Prot 44 g; Carbo 17 g; T Fat 13 g;
31% Calories from Fat; Chol 128 mg;
Fiber 1 g; Sod 1241 mg

Patricia A. Warner

1 (4- to 5-pound) beef
   brisket
2 teaspoons salt
¹/₂ teaspoon freshly
   ground pepper, or to
   taste
2 (or more) onions, sliced
4 ribs (or more) celery
2 cups chili sauce
¹/₂ cup water
1 (12-ounce) can beer

73

Old–Fashioned Southern Beef Brisket

Carol Spengler

1 (4- to 6-pound) beef
   brisket
1/2 cup low-sodium soy
   sauce
1/2 cup liquid smoke
2 cups (about) packed
   brown sugar
2 to 3 tablespoons
   vinegar, or to taste
2 to 3 tablespoons
   Worcestershire sauce,
   or to taste

P lace the brisket in a baking pan. Pour a
   mixture of the soy sauce and liquid
smoke over the beef.

❖ Bake, covered, at 325 degrees for at
least 2 hours per pound or until tender,
basting occasionally.

❖ Drain off most of the pan drippings.
Cut the beef into thin slices.

❖ Mix the brown sugar, vinegar and
Worcestershire sauce in a bowl. Pour
over the beef slices in the baking pan.
Bake at 300 to 325 degrees for 30 to
60 minutes or to desired degree of
doneness.

❖ Yield: 10 servings

Approx Per Serving:
Cal 501; Prot 52 g; Carbo 38 g; T Fat 15 g;
28% Calories from Fat; Chol 154 mg;
Fiber 0 g; Sod 187 mg

Main Dishes

Flank Steak Gulf Coast

Chair, Department of Obstetrics and Gynecology, Dr. Johnson is a local and national leader in women's health services and a strong supporter of maternal and child health. He enjoys providing both primary care at one of our satellite clinics and high risk care at our Women's Hospital.

Combine the oil, Worcestershire sauce, 1 teaspoon of the pepper, parsley, lemon juice, soy sauce, dry mustard, vinegar and onion salt in a bowl and mix well. Add the steak. Marinate in the refrigerator for 12 to 24 hours. Discard the marinade.

❖ Sauté the green onions, green pepper, celery, garlic and parsley in the butter in a skillet. Add the crab meat and shrimp. Sauté until the shrimp turn pink. Add the bread crumbs, salt and remaining 1/2 teaspoon pepper. Stir in enough sherry to moisten.

❖ Spread the shrimp mixture over the steak. Roll as for a jelly roll and tie securely. Place in a baking pan.

❖ Bake, covered with foil, at 350 degrees for 50 minutes.

❖ Cut into slices. Serve hot.

❖ Yield: 6 servings

Approx Per Serving:
Cal 567; Prot 48 g; Carbo 20 g; T Fat 32 g; 50% Calories from Fat; Chol 224 mg; Fiber 1 g; Sod 2605 mg

Timothy Johnson, M.D.

1/3 cup vegetable oil
1/4 cup Worcestershire sauce
1 1/2 teaspoons pepper
1 1/2 teaspoons parsley flakes
1/3 cup lemon juice
1/2 cup soy sauce
2 tablespoons dry mustard
1/2 cup wine vinegar
1 teaspoon onion salt
1 (2-pound) flank steak
1 bunch green onions, finely chopped
1 small green or red bell pepper, finely chopped
2 ribs celery, finely chopped
1 clove of garlic, minced
1/4 cup minced parsley
1/4 cup butter
8 ounces crab meat
1 pound shrimp, peeled, deveined
3/4 cup bread crumbs
1 teaspoon salt
1/4 to 1/2 cup sherry

75

Main Dishes

Border Shepherd's Pie

John Temple

1 1/2 pounds potatoes
1 pound minced beef
2 large onions, chopped
1/2 green bell pepper,
    chopped
4 ounces mushrooms,
    chopped
3 to 4 tomatoes, chopped
Worcestershire sauce to
    taste
Salt and pepper to taste
1/4 cup butter
2 tablespoons hot milk

John, a corporate VP for Northwest Airlines, has been an important advocate for our children's hospital for several years.

Boil the potatoes in water to cover in a saucepan until tender.

❖ Combine the beef and onions in a large nonstick skillet. Add the green pepper, mushrooms, tomatoes, Worcestershire sauce, salt and pepper and mix well. Sauté until the vegetables are tender. Spoon into a greased pie plate.

❖ Mash the potatoes well in a bowl. Add the butter and milk and mix well. Spread over the beef mixture. Press with a fork in a decorative pattern.

❖ Bake at 450 degrees for 20 to 30 minutes or until the top is golden brown and the mixture is heated through.

❖ May spoon the potato mixture into a pastry bag fitted with a large star tube and pipe over the beef mixture.

❖ Yield: 4 servings

Approx Per Serving:
Cal 576; Prot 31 g; Carbo 51 g; T Fat 28 g;
44% Calories from Fat; Chol 116 mg;
Fiber 6 g; Sod 205 mg

76

Main Dishes

Combine the ground chuck, cheese, 1 teaspoon dry mustard, pepper, chili sauce, Worcestershire sauce, cornflakes, milk and eggs in a bowl and mix well. Spread evenly in a loaf pan.

❖ Mix the brown sugar, catsup, nutmeg and 1 teaspoon dry mustard in a bowl. Spread over the meat loaf.

❖ Bake at 350 degrees for 1 hour. Cool for several minutes before serving.

❖ Yield: 8 servings

Approx Per Serving:
Cal 532; Prot 39 g; Carbo 26 g; T Fat 30 g; 51% Calories from Fat; Chol 179 mg; Fiber 1 g; Sod 700 mg

Patricia A. Warner

2 pounds ground chuck
2$^{1}/_{2}$ cups shredded sharp
    Cheddar cheese
1 teaspoon dry mustard
$^{1}/_{4}$ teaspoon pepper
3 tablespoons chili sauce
1 tablespoon
    Worcestershire sauce
2 cups crushed cornflakes
1 cup milk
2 eggs
3 tablespoons brown
    sugar
$^{1}/_{4}$ cup catsup
$^{1}/_{4}$ teaspoon nutmeg
1 teaspoon dry mustard

Italian Meat Loaf

Joe and Carolyn Roberson

3/4 cup cracker crumbs
1 cup milk
2 eggs
1/2 cup ground Parmesan
   or Romano cheese
1/4 cup chopped green
   bell pepper
1/4 cup chopped onion
1 tablespoon
   Worcestershire sauce
1 teaspoon basil
Salt and garlic powder to
   taste
1 1/2 pounds ground
   sirloin
1/4 to 1/2 cup catsup

Joe is the University of Michigan Athletic Director and has been very supportive of our hospital.

Soak the crackers in the milk in a small bowl.

❖ Beat the eggs with a fork in a medium bowl. Add the milk mixture, cheese, green pepper, onion, Worcestershire sauce, basil, salt and garlic powder and mix well.

❖ Combine the ground sirloin and egg mixture in a large bowl and mix lightly. Shape into a loaf. Place in a 5x10-inch loaf pan. Drizzle the catsup over the meat loaf.

❖ Bake at 350 degrees for 1 1/2 hours.

❖ Serve with additional catsup.

❖ Yield: 6 servings

Approx Per Serving:
Cal 331; Prot 34 g; Carbo 17 g; T Fat 14 g; 38% Calories from Fat; Chol 159 mg; Fiber 1 g; Sod 659 mg

78

Main Dishes

Upper Peninsula Pasties

This originated in Cornwall, England, and was brought to Michigan U.P. by the Cornish people. The women used to make these and bring them to their husbands working at the mines for lunch. The original recipe also called for rutabaga in small pieces.

B ring the water and salt to a boil in a saucepan. Add the shortening. Let cool. Stir in the flour; do not knead. Chill for 4 hours to overnight.

❖ Divide the dough into 7 balls. Knead on a lightly floured surface. Roll to the size of dinner plates.

❖ Mix the potatoes, onion, ground round and butter in a bowl. Add salt, pepper and seasoned salt.

❖ Fill each piece of dough with 1 heaping cup of the meat mixture. Fold over into the shape of a half moon. Brush with the egg.

❖ Place in a baking pan or on a nonstick baking sheet. Bake at 375 to 400 degrees for 45 minutes or until lightly browned.

❖ Yield: 7 servings

Approx Per Serving:
Cal 885; Prot 32 g; Carbo 75 g; T Fat 51 g;
52% Calories from Fat; Chol 120 mg;
Fiber 5 g; Sod 445 mg

Sandy Knight

1 cup water
1 teaspoon salt
1 cup shortening
3 cups flour
8 1/2 cups finely chopped
    potatoes
1 medium onion,
    chopped
1 1/2 pounds ground
    round
1/4 cup melted butter
Salt, pepper and seasoned
    salt to taste
1 egg, beaten

79

Main Dishes

Tacoritos

Diane Shember

2 pounds ground beef
1 medium onion,
　　chopped
1 teaspoon chili powder
1 teaspoon garlic powder
1 teaspoon salt
1 teaspoon pepper
2 (10-ounce) cans
　　Cheddar cheese soup
1 (10-ounce) can cream of
　　chicken soup
1 cup water
1 teaspoon cumin
1 teaspoon oregano
10 flour tortillas
2 1/2 to 3 cups shredded
　　lettuce
2 1/2 to 3 cups chopped
　　tomatoes
1/4 to 1/2 cup shredded
　　Cheddar cheese

Brown the ground beef with the onion in a skillet, stirring until the ground beef is crumbly; drain well. Add the chili powder, garlic powder, salt and pepper and mix well.

❖ Combine the soups, water, cumin and oregano in a saucepan. Simmer for 30 minutes.

❖ Spoon the ground beef mixture onto the tortillas. Top each with 1 tablespoon of the soup mixture. Add the lettuce and tomatoes. Roll up and place seam side down in 1 large casserole or 2 flat casseroles sprayed with nonstick cooking spray. Cover with the remaining soup mixture. Sprinkle with the cheese.

❖ Bake at 350 degrees until bubbly and heated through.

❖ May be prepared ahead and frozen for later use.

❖ Yield: 10 servings

Approx Per Serving:
Cal 458; Prot 29 g; Carbo 31 g; T Fat 24 g;
47% Calories from Fat; Chol 90 mg;
Fiber 2 g; Sod 1178 mg

Vegetables & Side Dishes

C. S. MOTT CHILDREN'S HOSPITAL

John and Mary Lou Dasburg

John Dasburg is President and CEO of Northwest Airlines, Inc. Northwest Airlines has been a major supporter of C.S. Mott Children's Hospital since 1988. Flight attendants have volunteered their time at several of our fundraisers. Pilots and ground personnel have distributed toys to the patients at Mott during Christmas. Through the generosity of regional and corporate executives from Northwest Airlines, we have been able to raise more than $100,000. Thank you Northwest Airlines for taking a leadership role in supporting C.S. Mott Children's Hospital.

Red Sauce

Sauté the garlic in the olive oil in a large heavy saucepan. Add the onion. Sauté until tender. Add the red bell peppers, tomato sauce and stewed tomatoes.

❖ Bring to a boil; reduce the heat to low. Stir in the oregano, thyme, basil, fennel seeds and pepper.

❖ Serve the sauce over pasta. May add mushrooms or Italian sausage.

❖ Yield: 6 servings

Approx Per Serving:
Cal 173; Prot 2 g; Carbo 18 g; T Fat 11 g;
56% Calories from Fat; Chol 0 mg;
Fiber 4 g; Sod 876 mg

John and Mary Lou Dasburg

1/4 cup minced garlic
5 tablespoons extra-virgin olive oil
1 onion, finely chopped
1 cup chopped roasted red bell peppers
1 (8-ounce) can tomato sauce
2 (15-ounce) cans stewed Italian tomatoes
1 teaspoon oregano
1 teaspoon thyme
1 teaspoon basil
1 teaspoon fennel seeds
Pepper to taste

Vegetables & Side Dishes

Jack and Mary Lou's Teriyaki Marinade

Jack's legendary political commentary is heard on several radio and television stations in Detroit. Mary Lou has taught journalism at Michigan and was recently inducted into the Michigan Women's Hall of Fame.

Combine the teriyaki marinade, mustard, Worcestershire sauce, balsamic vinegar and salad dressing in a bowl. Mix thoroughly. Stir in the garlic pepper, basil, rosemary, seasoned salt and lemon juice. Store in a covered container in the refrigerator until ready to use.

❖ Spoon the marinade over steaks 30 minutes before grilling, or place steaks in a sealable plastic bag with the marinade, turning to cover.

❖ Yield: 3 ($^1/_2$-cup) servings

Approx Per Serving:
Cal 187; Prot 6 g; Carbo 24 g; T Fat 9 g; 39% Calories from Fat; Chol 0 mg; Fiber 1 g; Sod 4338 mg

*Jack Casey and
Mary Lou Butcher*

6 ounces teriyaki
    marinade and base
3 ounces Dijon mustard
1$^1/_2$ tablespoons
    Worcestershire sauce
2 tablespoons balsamic
    vinegar
1 ounce Italian salad
    dressing
2 tablespoons garlic
    pepper
1 tablespoon dried basil
1 tablespoon dried
    rosemary
1 tablespoon seasoned
    salt
1 tablespoon lemon juice

85

Vegetables & Side Dishes

Stuffed Acorn Squash

Molly Walsh

1 acorn squash
6 ounces ground pork or
   turkey
1/4 cup chopped celery
1/4 cup chopped onion
1/4 teaspoon salt
1/4 teaspoon curry
   powder
1/4 teaspoon cinnamon
1/2 cup unsweetened
   applesauce
1 slice raisin bread, cubed

Cut the squash into halves. Remove and discard seeds. Place cut side down in a 6x10-inch baking dish sprayed with non-stick cooking spray. Bake at 350 degrees for 50 minutes.

❖ Brown the pork, celery and onion in a large skillet until the pork is cooked through, stirring frequently; drain well.

❖ Stir in the salt, curry powder and cinnamon. Cook for 1 minute. Add the applesauce and bread cubes.

❖ Spoon the mixture into each squash half. Bake for 20 minutes longer. Serve immediately.

❖ Yield: 2 servings

Approx Per Serving:
Cal 374; Prot 20 g; Carbo 46 g; T Fat 14 g;
33% Calories from Fat; Chol 60 mg;
Fiber 11 g; Sod 385 mg

86

Suzanne's Asparagus Tart

Line a 9-inch pie plate with the pastry. Prick the surface with a fork.

❖ Cut the asparagus into 2-inch pieces. Arrange in the prepared pie plate. Pour the cream over the asparagus.

❖ Beat the egg yolks and the egg in a small bowl. Pour over the asparagus. Cover with the cheese; season with salt and pepper.

❖ Bake at 375 degrees for 20 to 30 minutes or until lightly browned and set.

❖ Yield: 6 servings

Approx Per Serving:
Cal 422; Prot 10 g; Carbo 19 g; T Fat 34 g;
73% Calories from Fat; Chol 226 mg;
Fiber <1 g; Sod 280 mg

Suzanne Grousset

1 all ready pie pastry
1 bunch fresh asparagus, trimmed
1 cup whipping cream
3 egg yolks
1 egg
4 ounces Gruyère cheese, shredded
Salt and pepper to taste

87

Vegetables & Side Dishes

Cuban Black Beans

Betty Kelsch

1 pound black turtle
 beans
1 large green bell pepper,
 coarsely chopped
1 large onion, coarsely
 chopped
1 teaspoon olive oil
1 teaspoon salt
1 tablespoon cumin
2 tablespoons apple cider
 vinegar

Rinse and sort the beans. Soak the beans in water to cover for 8 to 10 hours; drain. Place the beans in a large saucepan with water to cover.

❖ Bring to a boil; reduce heat. Simmer, covered, for 2 to 3 hours or until the beans are tender.

❖ Sauté the green pepper and onion in the olive oil in a nonstick skillet for 2 minutes. Add to the beans. Stir in the salt, cumin and vinegar. Simmer over low heat until the liquid is thickened.

❖ Serve over rice.

❖ Yield: 10 servings

Approx Per Serving:
Cal 168; Prot 11 g; Carbo 30 g; T Fat 1 g;
6% Calories from Fat; Chol 0 mg;
Fiber 10 g; Sod 220 mg

Vegetables & Side Dishes

Green Beans and Brown Rice

Rinse the rice well; drain. Place in a heavy saucepan with the chicken stock and 1/4 teaspoon salt. Bring to a boil; reduce heat to low. Cook, covered, for 45 minutes or until all the liquid is absorbed. Do not stir. Fluff with a fork when done.

❖ Fill a large saucepan 3/4 full of lightly salted water. Bring to a boil. Add the green beans. Cook for 5 to 7 minutes or until tender-crisp; drain well. Combine with the rice and peanuts in a large bowl.

❖ Combine the mustard, garlic, rice vinegar, soy sauce, sesame oil, corn oil and pepper in a small bowl. Whisk briskly until slightly thickened. Pour over the rice and bean mixture, tossing to coat.

❖ Toast the sesame seeds in a skillet over medium heat for 2 to 3 minutes, stirring constantly. Sprinkle over the rice mixture and serve at once.

❖ Yield: 6 servings

Approx Per Serving:
Cal 231; Prot 8 g; Carbo 22 g; T Fat 14 g;
51% Calories from Fat; Chol 0 mg;
Fiber 5 g; Sod 593 mg

Peter Murchie

1/2 cup brown rice
1 cup chicken or
    vegetable stock or
    water
1/4 teaspoon salt
Salt to taste
11/4 pounds green beans,
    trimmed and sliced
    diagonally into 11/2-
    inch pieces
1/2 cup raw peanuts,
    toasted
1 teaspoon Dijon mustard
1 clove of garlic, minced
11/2 tablespoons rice
    vinegar or fresh lemon
    juice
2 tablespoons soy sauce
2 teaspoons sesame oil
2 tablespoons corn oil
Freshly ground pepper to
    taste
1 tablespoon sesame
    seeds

89

Vegetables & Side Dishes

Broccoli Casserole

Nell Fallon

1/4 cup chopped onion
4 teaspoons butter
2 teaspoons flour
2 (10-ounce) packages
    frozen chopped
    broccoli, thawed,
    drained
1/2 cup water
1 (8-ounce) jar Cheez
    Whiz
3 eggs, beaten
1/2 cup dry bread crumbs
2 teaspoons melted butter

Sauté the onion in 4 teaspoons butter in a large skillet. Sprinkle with the flour, stirring well. Add the broccoli, water and Cheez Whiz.

❖ Simmer over low heat until the cheese is melted, stirring frequently. Remove from the heat; cool. Add the eggs slowly, stirring constantly to incorporate. Pour into a greased 2-quart baking dish.

❖ Toss the bread crumbs with the 2 teaspoons melted butter. Sprinkle over the broccoli mixture.

❖ Bake at 350 degrees for 45 minutes.

❖ Yield: 6 servings

Approx Per Serving:
Cal 246; Prot 14 g; Carbo 16 g; T Fat 15 g;
53% Calories from Fat; Chol 137 mg;
Fiber 3 g; Sod 672 mg

Vegetables & Side Dishes

Ginger Carrots

Combine the sugar, orange juice, broth, margarine, lemon peel, ginger and cloves in a heavy saucepan.

❖ Simmer for 10 minutes, stirring occasionally. Add the carrots.

❖ Simmer for 10 to 15 minutes or until the carrots are tender-crisp. Remove the cloves before serving.

❖ Yield: 4 servings

Approx Per Serving:
Cal 138; Prot 1 g; Carbo 32 g; T Fat 1 g;
9% Calories from Fat; Chol 0 mg;
Fiber 2 g; Sod 81 mg

Dara Gaucher

1/2 cup sugar
1/4 cup fresh orange juice
1/4 cup chicken broth
1 teaspoon margarine
Grated peel of 1 lemon
1/2 teaspoon ground
    ginger
5 whole cloves
1 bunch tiny carrots,
    trimmed and peeled

91

Pan de Elote (Bread and Corn Pudding)

*Robert and
Kathryn Altman*

1 (16-ounce) can cream-
    style corn
2 tablespoons melted
    butter
1 cup baking mix
1 egg, beaten
1/2 cup milk
1 (4-ounce) can chopped
    green chiles, drained
8 ounces Monterey Jack
    cheese, thinly sliced

*Artist-in-residence and famous Hollywood
writer, Robert Altman is producer and director of such classics as* Short Cuts, Nashville
and M*A*S*H.

Combine the corn, butter, baking mix,
egg and milk in a medium bowl,
mixing well.

❖ Pour half of the corn mixture into a
greased 8-inch square baking dish. Layer
with the chiles and cheese slices. Top
with the remaining mixture.

❖ Bake at 400 degrees for 20 minutes or
until browned.

❖ Yield: 6 servings

Approx Per Serving:
Cal 340; Prot 14 g; Carbo 28 g; T Fat 20 g;
53% Calories from Fat; Chol 83 mg;
Fiber 1 g; Sod 965 mg

Vegetables & Side Dishes

Marinated Button Mushrooms

Slice the lemon very thinly. Remove the seeds and cut each slice into quarters; set aside.

❖ Remove and discard the stem and seeds of the red pepper. Cut the pepper into 3/8-inch squares; set aside.

❖ Combine the wine and vinegar in a large stainless steel saucepan. Add the salt, pepper, chile pepper, oregano, cloves, parsley, garlic, lemon quarters and pepper squares. Bring to a boil.

❖ Add the mushrooms; sprinkle with the olive oil. Boil for 7 minutes, stirring occasionally. Remove from the heat; cool.

❖ Spoon into a serving bowl and serve at room temperature.

❖ Yield: 4 servings

Approx Per Serving:
Cal 165; Prot 3 g; Carbo 12 g; T Fat 11 g;
53% Calories from Fat; Chol 0 mg;
Fiber 2 g; Sod 542 mg

Nellie Wolgast

1 lemon
1 small red sweet pepper
   (capiscum)
2/3 cup dry white wine
2/3 cup rice vinegar
1 teaspoon fine sea salt
1 teaspoon coarsely
   ground pepper
1 dried hot chile pepper,
   crumbled
2 teaspoons dried
   oregano
3 whole cloves
2 tablespoons snipped
   fresh parsley
1 clove of garlic, minced
1 pound tiny button
   mushrooms, stems
   trimmed
3 tablespoons extra-virgin
   olive oil

93

Vegetables & Side Dishes

Mushrooms au Gratin

Lynn O'Neal

1 large onion, chopped
1 clove of garlic, minced
1/4 cup butter
1 1/2 pounds mushrooms,
    sliced
Salt and pepper to taste
1 1/4 cups crème fraîche
1 tablespoon dry bread
    crumbs
1 tablespoon grated
    Parmesan cheese
1 tablespoon butter

Sauté the onion and garlic in 1/4 cup butter in a large heavy skillet. Add the mushrooms. Simmer, covered, until the mushrooms are tender. Season with salt and pepper. Drain, reserving the pan juices.

❖ Bring the crème fraîche to a boil in a small saucepan. Add the reserved mushroom juices. Simmer gently until thickened, stirring frequently. Fold in the mushrooms.

❖ Spoon the mixture into 4 buttered ramekins. Sprinkle with the bread crumbs and cheese. Dot with the remaining 1 tablespoon butter. Broil until browned. Serve immediately.

❖ Note: To make crème fraîche, mix 1 cup whipping cream with 1 teaspoon cultured buttermilk in a saucepan. Heat gently until thickened, stirring occasionally. Chill until needed.

❖ Yield: 4 servings

Approx Per Serving:
Cal 456; Prot 7 g; Carbo 15 g; T Fat 43 g; 82% Calories from Fat; Chol 142 mg; Fiber 3 g; Sod 227 mg

94

Combine the muffin mix, egg, milk, corn and Tabasco sauce in a bowl; mix well. Pour into a greased baking dish.

❖ Sauté the onion in the butter in a large skillet until tender. Stir in the sour cream, salt, dillweed and half of the cheese. Spread the mixture over the batter. Sprinkle with the remaining 1/2 cup cheese.

❖ Bake at 425 degrees for 25 to 30 minutes or until browned and bubbly.

❖ Yield: 6 servings

Approx Per Serving:
Cal 428; Prot 11 g; Carbo 41 g; T Fat 26 g;
53% Calories from Fat; Chol 95 mg;
Fiber 1 g; Sod 747 mg

Christine Berry

1 1/2 cups corn muffin mix
1 egg, beaten
1/3 cup milk
1 (16-ounce) can cream-
    style corn
2 drops of Tabasco sauce
1 sweet Spanish onion,
    sliced
1/4 cup butter
1 cup sour cream
1/4 teaspoon salt
1/4 teaspoon dillweed
1 cup shredded sharp
    Cheddar cheese

95

Vegetables & Side Dishes

Spicy Peperonata

Bob Hilty

8 red, yellow and green
    bell peppers
2 medium red onions,
    coarsely chopped
2 cloves of garlic, coarsely
    chopped
1/2 cup olive oil
Salt and freshly ground
    black pepper to taste
1/2 teaspoon hot red
    pepper flakes
5 tablespoons (heaping)
    wine-vinegar-pack
    capers, drained
20 sprigs of Italian
    parsley, leaves only,
    coarsely chopped

Remove and discard the stems and seeds of the peppers. Cut into 1/2-inch wide strips. Soak in cold water in a bowl for 30 minutes.

❖ Sauté the onions and garlic in the olive oil in a skillet over medium heat for 20 minutes, stirring occasionally.

❖ Drain the peppers. Add to the onion mixture. Season with salt, black pepper and red pepper. Sauté for 5 minutes over high heat, stirring constantly. Reduce the heat to low.

❖ Cook, covered, for 15 minutes or until the peppers are cooked through but firm, stirring occasionally.

❖ Rinse the capers. Add to the skillet. Simmer for 2 minutes longer.

❖ Spoon onto a warmed large serving platter. Sprinkle with the parsley. Serve hot or at room temperature.

❖ Yield: 8 servings

Approx Per Serving:
Cal 151; Prot 1 g; Carbo 7 g; T Fat 14 g;
79% Calories from Fat; Chol 0 mg;
Fiber 2 g; Sod 200 mg

96

Vegetables & Side Dishes

Campfire Potatoes

Arrange the potato and onion slices on a large sheet of heavy-duty foil. Dot with the butter.

❖ Sprinkle evenly with a mixture of the Worcestershire sauce, salt and pepper. Top with the cheese and parsley.

❖ Pour the chicken broth over the mixture. Fold up the foil, sealing the edges to enclose.

❖ Grill over medium-hot coals for 35 to 40 minutes, turning the foil package every 15 minutes.

❖ May substitute margarine for the butter.

❖ Yield: 6 servings

Approx Per Serving:
Cal 232; Prot 4 g; Carbo 24 g; T Fat 14 g; 52% Calories from Fat; Chol 38 mg; Fiber 2 g; Sod 233 mg

Maggie Brownridge

5 medium potatoes,
    peeled, thinly sliced
1 medium onion, sliced
6 tablespoons butter
1 tablespoon
    Worcestershire sauce
Salt and pepper to taste
1/3 cup shredded
    Cheddar cheese
2 tablespoons minced
    parsley
1/3 cup chicken broth

97

Vegetables & Side Dishes

German-Style Potato Pancakes

Carole F. Dubritsky

2 tablespoons flour
1 teaspoon salt
1/4 teaspoon baking
     powder
1/2 teaspoon pepper
2 eggs, beaten
1 small yellow onion,
     grated
6 medium potatoes,
     peeled, grated, drained
Vegetable oil for frying

Combine the flour, salt, baking powder and pepper in a bowl. Add the eggs, beating well. Mix in the onion and potatoes.

❖ Spoon 2 to 3 tablespoons of the mixture into a hot lightly greased 10-inch skillet. Cook until brown on both sides, turning only once. Repeat with the remaining mixture.

❖ Serve plain or with sour cream or applesauce.

❖ Yield: 5 servings

Approx Per Serving:
Cal 182; Prot 6 g; Carbo 35 g; T Fat 2 g;
11% Calories from Fat; Chol 85 mg;
Fiber 3 g; Sod 476 mg
Nutritional profile does not include
oil for frying.

98

Vegetables & Side Dishes

Rice Pilaf

Melt the margarine in a large deep skillet. Add the onion, rice and soup mix. Sauté until the onion is tender and the rice is browned.

❖ Pour in the chicken broth. Simmer, covered, until all the liquid is absorbed.

❖ Yield: 8 servings

Approx Per Serving:
Cal 196; Prot 4 g; Carbo 29 g; T Fat 6 g;
30% Calories from Fat; Chol <1 mg;
Fiber 1 g; Sod 391 mg

Carolyn Benson

1/4 cup margarine
1/2 cup chopped onion
1 1/2 cups rice
1 envelope onion soup
      mix
2 1/2 cups chicken broth

Spinach Casserole

Thaw the spinach at room temperature or in the microwave. Drain well.

❖ Combine the spinach and cottage cheese in a medium bowl. Add the eggs, flour, margarine and Velveeta cheese. Mix thoroughly. Spoon into a greased baking dish.

❖ Bake at 350 degrees for 1 hour.

❖ Yield: 8 servings

Approx Per Serving:
Cal 368; Prot 28 g; Carbo 11 g; T Fat 24 g;
58% Calories from Fat; Chol 203 mg;
Fiber 2 g; Sod 1031 mg

Rosanne Whitehouse

2 (10-ounce) packages
      frozen chopped
      spinach
32 ounces small curd
      cottage cheese,
      drained
6 eggs, beaten
6 tablespoons flour
1/4 cup margarine, cut
      into pieces
8 ounces Velveeta cheese,
      cubed

99

Morel and Asparagus Risotto

Prue Rosenthal

6 thick asparagus spears,
    peeled
1 tablespoon unsalted
    butter
6 ounces morel or cremini
    mushrooms, cleaned,
    cut into bite-size pieces
1/4 teaspoon kosher salt
Freshly ground pepper to
    taste
8 cups (about) chicken
    broth
2 tablespoons unsalted
    butter
2 tablespoons olive oil
4 shallots, peeled, minced
1 clove of garlic, minced
1 (16-ounce) package
    arborio rice
1/2 cup dry white wine
1/4 cup cooked tiny peas
3 tablespoons minced
    fresh chives
1 tablespoon unsalted
    butter
2 teaspoons kosher salt
1/4 cup fresh chervil
    leaves

Cook the asparagus in water to cover in a saucepan until tender. Cut diagonally into 1/4-inch slices and set aside.

❖ Heat 1 tablespoon butter in a skillet over medium heat. Add the mushrooms. Sauté for 10 minutes or until tender. Add 1/4 teaspoon salt and pepper.

❖ Bring the broth to a boil in a saucepan. Reduce heat and keep at a low simmer.

❖ Heat 2 tablespoons butter and olive oil in a large saucepan over medium-low heat. Add the shallots and garlic. Sauté for 5 minutes or until tender. Add the rice, stirring with a wooden spoon until coated. Cook for 4 minutes, stirring constantly. Stir in the wine. Increase the heat to medium. Cook for 1 minute or until the wine is absorbed.

❖ Add the broth 1/2 cup at a time, stirring constantly and adding more broth as it is absorbed by the rice. Adjust the heat so that the rice and broth remain at a steady simmer. The rice should be tender and some broth should remain after about 15 minutes.

❖ Cook for several minutes or until the rice is al dente, adding broth as needed. Stir in the asparagus, mushrooms, peas, chives and 1 tablespoon butter. Add 2 teaspoons salt and pepper to taste.

❖ Divide among 6 shallow bowls. Top with the chervil.

❖ Yield: 6 servings

Approx Per Serving:
Cal 504; Prot 15 g; Carbo 74 g; T Fat 15 g;
27% Calories from Fat; Chol 21 mg;
Fiber 2 g; Sod 1848 mg

100

Risotto alla Milanese

Coach Fisher, the Michigan head basketball coach, has visited Mott Children's Hospital on several occasions. He also donates a portion of the revenues from his summer basketball camp to Mott each year.

Melt 5 tablespoons butter in a 4-quart saucepan over medium heat. Add the onion. Cook until transparent but not browned.

❖ Add the wine. Cook over high heat until the liquid is evaporated.

❖ Add the rice. Season with salt and pepper. Stir until the grains are coated with the butter. Add the saffron and 2 cups of the chicken broth.

❖ Simmer until the liquid is almost absorbed. Add the remaining broth a small amount at a time, cooking until the liquid is almost absorbed before each addition. Reduce the heat.

❖ Cook, uncovered, for 20 to 25 minutes longer or until the rice is al dente, stirring frequently. Remove from the heat. Stir in the remaining 3 tablespoons butter and half the cheese.

❖ Serve immediately with the remaining cheese.

❖ Yield: 8 servings

Approx Per Serving:
Cal 375; Prot 12 g; Carbo 39 g; T Fat 16 g;
40% Calories from Fat; Chol 41 mg;
Fiber 1 g; Sod 1105 mg

Steve and Angie Fisher

5 tablespoons butter
1 small onion, finely
    chopped
1 cup dry white wine
2 cups long grain white
    rice
1 teaspoon salt
1/4 teaspoon white pepper
1/2 teaspoon saffron
    threads
5 cups chicken broth
3 tablespoons butter
1 cup freshly grated
    Parmesan cheese

Vegetables & Side Dishes

Tomatoes Florentine

Erica Gaucher

6 medium tomatoes
2 tablespoons margarine
1 small onion, finely
    chopped
1 clove of garlic, minced
1 (10-ounce) package
    frozen chopped
    spinach, thawed and
    drained
1/3 cup 1% milk
Salt and freshly ground
    pepper to taste
2 tablespoons fine dry
    bread crumbs
2 tablespoons chopped
    fresh parsley
2 tablespoons grated
    Parmesan cheese

Slice the tops off the tomatoes. Scoop out half the pulp from each tomato and discard or save for sauces or soups. Set the tomato shells aside.

❖ Melt the margarine in a skillet over medium heat. Add the onion and garlic. Sauté until tender.

❖ Add the spinach, milk, salt and pepper; mix well. Spoon the mixture into the tomato shells. Place in a greased baking dish. Sprinkle with a mixture of the bread crumbs, parsley and cheese.

❖ Bake at 400 degrees for 20 minutes or until heated through and browned.

❖ Yield: 6 servings

Approx Per Serving:
Cal 100; Prot 4 g; Carbo 11 g; T Fat 5 g;
44% Calories from Fat; Chol 2 mg;
Fiber 3 g; Sod 155 mg

102

Easy Veggie Lasagna

Prepare the noodles using the package directions; drain well.

❖ Combine the ricotta cheese, spinach, 1/2 cup of the mozzarella cheese, Parmesan cheese and eggs in a medium bowl and mix well.

❖ Layer 2 cups of the spaghetti sauce, half the noodles, half the remaining sauce, all the spinach mixture, half the remaining mozzarella cheese, remaining noodles and remaining sauce in a 9x15-inch baking pan.

❖ Bake, covered, at 350 degrees for 45 minutes or until bubbly.

❖ Top with the remaining mozzarella cheese and parsley. Bake, uncovered, for 15 minutes.

❖ Let stand for 10 minutes before serving. Store leftovers in the refrigerator.

❖ Yield: 12 servings

Approx Per Serving:
Cal 389; Prot 23 g; Carbo 37 g; T Fat 17 g;
40% Calories from Fat; Chol 69 mg;
Fiber 3 g; Sod 987 mg

Sylvia Ertman

8 ounces lasagna noodles
15 ounces low-fat ricotta cheese
1 (10-ounce) package frozen chopped spinach, thawed, drained
1 pound low-fat mozzarella cheese, shredded
1/2 cup grated low-fat Parmesan cheese
2 eggs, beaten
2 (26-ounce) jars spaghetti sauce
Chopped parsley to taste

Pasta with Cannellini and Tomatoes

Jeri Kelch

4 ounces thinly sliced
    ham
1 tablespoon olive oil
2 medium cloves of garlic,
    finely chopped
1 small onion, minced
1/3 cup chicken stock
1 (16-ounce) can salt-free
    tomatoes, chopped
1 cup drained, rinsed
    canned cannellini
1 tablespoon double
    concentrate tomato
    paste
1 tablespoon finely
    chopped fresh savory
    leaves
1 tablespoon finely
    chopped fresh basil
    leaves
1 tablespoon finely
    chopped fresh Italian
    parsley
2 teaspoons sugar
1 teaspoon dried oregano
8 ounces fettuccini or
    penne, cooked,
    drained

Robert C. Kelch, M.D., was Chair of Pediatrics from 1981 to 1994. Currently he is Dean, School of Medicine, University of Iowa. Bob and Jeri have been and remain Michigan fans with particular love and support for Mott Hospital.

Cut the ham into 1/4x1-inch strips. Heat the olive oil in a skillet. Add the garlic, onion and ham. Cook for 3 to 5 minutes or until the garlic and onion begin to brown.

❖ Add the chicken stock, stirring to deglaze the skillet. Add the tomatoes. Stir in the cannellini, tomato paste, savory, basil, parsley, sugar and oregano.

❖ Simmer for 15 minutes or until the sauce is thicker but still slightly liquid.

❖ Spoon over the hot pasta.

❖ Yield: 4 servings

Approx Per Serving:
Cal 389; Prot 20 g; Carbo 63 g; T Fat 7 g;
15% Calories from Fat; Chol 16 mg;
Fiber 7 g; Sod 748 mg

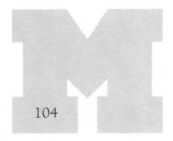

Vegetables & Side Dishes

Pasta with Michigan Morels

Professor of Film and Video at Michigan and author of the recent book, "Oliver Stone: Wake Up Cinema," Frank helped in obtaining some of the recipes for the book from Michigan alumni and friends in Hollywood.

Cook the pasta in boiling water with 1/2 teaspoon salt in a saucepan for 10 minutes or until al dente; drain well.

❖ Melt the butter in a cast-iron skillet over low heat. Add the shallots. Cook until tender. Add the mushrooms and 1 teaspoon salt. Cook for 10 minutes, stirring gently.

❖ Blend in the whipping cream and Cognac. Simmer for 5 minutes.

❖ Toss the morel sauce with the pasta. Sprinkle with the cheese, parsley and pepper.

❖ Arrange on 4 heated plates.

❖ Yield: 4 servings

Approx Per Serving:
Cal 577; Prot 18 g; Carbo 89 g; T Fat 15 g;
23% Calories from Fat; Chol 41 mg;
Fiber 4 g; Sod 874 mg

Frank Beaver

1 (16-ounce) package
    dried linguini or
    fettuccini
1/2 teaspoon salt
2 tablespoons unsalted
    butter
3 tablespoons chopped
    shallots or green
    onions
8 ounces Michigan morel
    mushrooms, cleaned
1 teaspoon salt
1/4 cup whipping cream
2 tablespoons Cognac
3 tablespoons grated
    Romano or Parmesan
    cheese
3 tablespoons chopped
    Italian parsley
Freshly ground pepper to
    taste

105

Vegetables & Side Dishes

Pasta with Portobello Mushrooms

Prue Rosenthal

1 pound fresh or dried
    pappardelle or
    fettuccini
2 tablespoons olive oil
6 shallots, finely minced
1/4 cup coarsely grated
    ginger
1 pound portobello
    mushrooms, cleaned,
    trimmed, sliced
1 1/4 cups reduced-fat
    ricotta cheese
1 1/4 cups nonfat plain
    yogurt
1 tablespoon cornstarch
1/4 teaspoon salt
Freshly ground pepper to
    taste
1/4 cup chopped parsley
1/2 cup coarsely grated
    Parmesan or Romano
    cheese

Cook the pasta in boiling water in a saucepan until tender; drain well.

❖ Heat the olive oil in a large skillet. Add the shallots, ginger and mushrooms. Cook until the mushrooms soften and release their liquid.

❖ Mix the ricotta cheese and yogurt in a bowl. Combine a small amount of the yogurt mixture with the cornstarch and mix to form a smooth paste; stir the cornstarch into the yogurt mixture.

❖ Reduce the heat under the mushroom mixture to very low. Stir in the yogurt mixture. Cook until warm but not hot; the mixture will separate if it becomes hot.

❖ Season with the salt and pepper. Spoon over the pasta. Sprinkle with the parsley.

❖ Serve with the cheese.

❖ May substitute an assortment of wild and common white mushrooms for the portobello mushrooms.

❖ Yield: 4 servings

Approx Per Serving:
Cal 813; Prot 38 g; Carbo 123 g; T Fat 19 g;
21% Calories from Fat; Chol 35 mg;
Fiber 5 g; Sod 550 mg

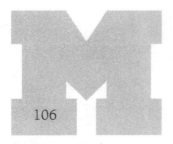

106

Brunch, Bread & Beverages

Trudy Bulkley

As Mother Goose, Trudy Bulkley presents monthly storytime programs at Kerrytown. She also appears for special occasions at C. S. Mott Children's Hospital. Old Mother Goose loves to wander, proud to be part of a tradition that know her "melodies will never die, while nurses sing or babies cry."

Jack Sprat Pancakes

Sift the flour, baking soda, salt and sugar into a large bowl. Mix the yogurt, skim milk and eggs in a medium bowl. Add to the flour mixture and mix well.

❖ Stir in the margarine. Beat until smooth, adding additional skim milk if a thinner pancake is desired.

❖ Heat a greased griddle or skillet until sprinkled water sizzles. Pour 1/4 cup of the batter per pancake onto the griddle. Bake until the entire pancake bubbles. Turn and bake until golden brown.

❖ Serve with maple syrup or other favorite syrup.

❖ A fun way to finish the final round of batter is to make pancake turtles: round body, 4 drops of batter for the feet and a slightly bigger drop for a head, plus a wisp of batter for a tail. Bake and turn as usual.

❖ Yield: 4 servings

Approx Per Serving:
Cal 242; Prot 9 g; Carbo 31 g; T Fat 9 g;
32% Calories from Fat; Chol 107 mg;
Fiber 1 g; Sod 610 mg

Trudy Bulkley
a.k.a. Mother Goose

1 cup flour
1 teaspoon baking soda
1/2 teaspoon salt
1 tablespoon sugar
1/2 cup nonfat yogurt
1/2 cup skim milk
2 eggs, beaten
2 tablespoons melted
    margarine, cooled

Brunch, Bread & Beverages

Marge's Apple Puff Pancakes

Heat a 12-inch ovenproof skillet in a 400-degree oven. Add the butter. Let the butter melt.

❖ Beat the eggs in a mixer bowl until frothy. Add the flour, milk and salt. Beat at medium speed for 1 minute.

❖ Mix the sugar and cinnamon in a bowl. Coat the apples with the sugar mixture.

❖ Arrange the apples in the skillet. Pour the batter over the apples.

❖ Bake at 400 degrees for 25 minutes.

❖ Yield: 2 servings

Approx Per Serving:
Cal 612; Prot 18 g; Carbo 72 g; T Fat 29 g; 42% Calories from Fat; Chol 377 mg; Fiber 4 g; Sod 849 mg

Joe Diederich

3 tablespoons butter
3 eggs
$3/4$ cup flour
$3/4$ cup milk
$1/2$ teaspoon salt
2 tablespoons sugar
$1/2$ teaspoon cinnamon
1 to 2 apples, thinly sliced

111

Brunch, Bread & Beverages

Bran Muffins

Nancy Lyke

5 cups flour
1 1/2 teaspoons salt
5 teaspoons baking soda
4 eggs
2 cups sugar
1 quart buttermilk
1 cup vegetable oil
1 (15-ounce) package
    Raisin Bran
1/2 (15-ounce) package
    raisins

Sift the flour, salt and baking soda together. Cream the eggs and sugar in a mixer bowl until light and fluffy. Add the flour mixture gradually, mixing well after each addition. Add the buttermilk, oil, cereal and raisins and mix well.

❖ Fill paper-lined muffin cups 3/4 full. Bake at 400 degrees for 20 minutes.

❖ May add 1 cup chopped pecans or walnuts to the batter.

❖ Yield: 48 servings

Approx Per Serving:
Cal 175; Prot 4 g; Carbo 29 g; T Fat 5 g;
27% Calories from Fat; Chol 18 mg;
Fiber 2 g; Sod 229 mg

Breakfast Casserole

Marilyn Hawkins

1 pound bulk sausage
6 slices white bread, torn
    into pieces
6 eggs
2 cups milk
1 cup shredded sharp
    Cheddar cheese

Brown the sausage in a skillet and drain. Place the bread in a greased 9x13-inch baking pan. Sprinkle with the sausage.

❖ Beat the eggs in a bowl. Stir in the milk. Pour over the sausage. Top with the cheese. Chill, covered, overnight.

❖ Bake at 350 degrees for 35 to 40 minutes or until heated through. Let stand for several minutes before slicing.

❖ May add 1 teaspoon dry mustard to the egg mixture.

❖ Yield: 10 servings

Approx Per Serving:
Cal 244; Prot 14 g; Carbo 12 g; T Fat 16 g;
58% Calories from Fat; Chol 164 mg;
Fiber <1 g; Sod 493 mg

112

Orange Muffins with Smoked Turkey

Dianne McNutt

Grind the raisins and orange zest in a food processor.

❖ Sift the flour and salt together.

❖ Dissolve the baking soda in the buttermilk.

❖ Cream 1 cup sugar and butter in a mixer bowl until light. Add the eggs and beat until fluffy. Add the flour mixture and buttermilk alternately, mixing well after each addition.

❖ Add the raisin mixture and mix well. Spoon into buttered small muffin cups.

❖ Bake at 400 degrees for 12 minutes or until golden brown and firm to the touch. Remove to a wire rack.

❖ Brush the tops of the warm muffins with the orange juice. Sprinkle with 1/2 cup sugar. Cool completely. Cut each muffin into halves.

❖ Place a small amount of turkey on each muffin half. Top with 1/2 teaspoon jelly.

❖ Yield: 30 servings

Approx Per Serving:
Cal 148; Prot 4 g; Carbo 26 g; T Fat 4 g;
24% Calories from Fat; Chol 26 mg;
Fiber 1 g; Sod 187 mg

1 cup raisins
Zest of 1 orange
2 cups sifted flour
1/2 teaspoon salt
1 teaspoon baking soda
1 cup buttermilk
1 cup sugar
1/2 cup unsalted butter, softened
2 eggs
Juice of 1 orange
1/2 cup sugar
8 ounces thinly sliced smoked turkey breast, cut into small pieces
3/4 cup quince jelly

113

Banana Bread

Betty Kelsch

1³/₄ cups sifted flour
2 teaspoons baking
    powder
¹/₄ teaspoon baking soda
¹/₂ teaspoon salt
¹/₃ cup unsweetened
    applesauce
²/₃ cup sugar
¹/₂ cup egg substitute, or
    the equivalent of 2
    eggs
1 cup mashed bananas

Sift the flour, baking powder, baking soda and salt together.

❖ Beat the applesauce and sugar in a mixer bowl. Add the egg substitute and beat well. Add the bananas and flour mixture alternately, beating until smooth after each addition.

❖ Pour into a 5x9-inch loaf pan sprayed with nonstick baking spray. Bake at 350 degrees for 1 hour and 10 minutes or until the loaf tests done.

❖ Cool in the pan for 10 minutes. Turn out on a wire rack to cool completely.

❖ May add 1 cup chopped walnuts to the batter.

❖ Yield: 12 servings

Approx Per Serving:
Cal 134; Prot 3 g; Carbo 29 g; T Fat 1 g;
4% Calories from Fat; Chol <1 mg;
Fiber 1 g; Sod 180 mg

114

Banana Chocolate Loaf

Cream the butter and sugar in a mixer bowl until light and fluffy. Add the eggs and salt and mix well.

❖ Dissolve the baking powder and baking soda in the yogurt. Add to the egg mixture and mix well. Stir in the bananas.

❖ Add the flour gradually, mixing well after each addition. Stir in the vanilla and chocolate chips.

❖ Pour into a 5x9-inch loaf pan sprayed with nonstick cooking spray. Bake at 350 degrees for 1 1/2 hours.

❖ Freezes well. May double the recipe, using 4 very ripe bananas and half the amount of chocolate chips. Bake in 4 miniature loaf pans sprayed with non-stick cooking spray.

❖ Yield: 12 servings

Approx Per Serving:
Cal 408; Prot 4 g; Carbo 61 g; T Fat 19 g; 40% Calories from Fat; Chol 57 mg; Fiber 2 g; Sod 275 mg

Marylen S. Oberman

1/2 cup butter, softened
1 2/3 cups sugar
2 eggs, slightly beaten
1/4 teaspoon salt
1 1/2 teaspoons baking
　　powder
1/2 teaspoon baking soda
1/4 cup nonfat yogurt or
　　sour cream
1 cup mashed bananas
2 cups cake flour, sifted
1 teaspoon vanilla extract
1 to 2 cups chocolate
　　chips

115

Lemon Nut Bread

Brenda Livingston

1¹/₂ cups flour
1 teaspoon salt
1 teaspoon baking
  powder
¹/₂ cup melted butter
1 cup sugar
2 eggs, beaten
1 tablespoon lemon
  extract
Grated zest of 1 lemon
¹/₂ cup milk
1 cup chopped walnuts or
  pecans
Juice of 1 lemon
2 cups confectioners'
  sugar

Combine the flour, salt and baking powder in a large bowl and mix well.

❖ Add the butter, sugar, eggs, flavoring and lemon zest and mix well. Stir in the milk and walnuts.

❖ Pour into a greased and floured loaf pan. Bake at 350 degrees for 50 minutes or until a wooden pick inserted near the center comes out clean.

❖ Bring the lemon juice to a boil in a saucepan over low heat. Add the confectioners' sugar and mix well. Boil for 5 minutes.

❖ Place the hot loaf on a serving plate. Pour the confectioners' sugar mixture over the loaf, spooning the excess over the loaf to coat the sides.

❖ Yield: 12 servings

Approx Per Serving:
Cal 362; Prot 5 g; Carbo 52 g; T Fat 15 g;
38% Calories from Fat; Chol 57 mg;
Fiber 1 g; Sod 300 mg

Pumpkin Nut Bread

Combine the pumpkin, oil, sugar, eggs and water in a large bowl and mix well. Add the flour gradually, mixing well after each addition.

❖ Add the nutmeg, cinnamon, salt and baking soda and mix well. Stir in the pecans.

❖ Pour into 2 greased loaf pans or 6 greased miniature foil loaf pans. Bake at 350 degrees for 1 hour or until the loaves test done.

❖ Cool in the pans. Remove and wrap in foil.

❖ Yield: 24 servings

Approx Per Serving:
Cal 329; Prot 4 g; Carbo 42 g; T Fat 17 g;
45% Calories from Fat; Chol 35 mg;
Fiber 2 g; Sod 214 mg

Brenda Livingston

2 cups solid-pack
    pumpkin
1 cup vegetable oil
3 cups sugar
4 eggs
2/3 cup water
3 1/2 cups flour
1 teaspoon nutmeg
1 teaspoon cinnamon
1 1/2 teaspoons salt
2 teaspoons baking soda
2 cups coarsely chopped
    pecans or walnuts

117

Brunch, Bread & Beverages

Jimmy Barrett's Monkey Bread

Jimmy Barrett

1/2 cup chopped pecans
1 (12-count) package
    frozen dinner rolls
3/4 cup packed brown
    sugar
1 teaspoon cinnamon
1 (4-ounce) package
    vanilla pudding and
    pie filling mix
6 tablespoons melted
    butter

Afternoon host at WXYT Radio, Jimmy has auctioned tickets to the Michigan/Ohio football games and raised thousands of dollars for our hospital.

Sprinkle the pecans in a greased bundt pan. Place the rolls in the pan with sides touching.

❖ Mix the brown sugar, cinnamon and pudding mix in a bowl. Sprinkle over the rolls. Spoon the butter over the rolls.

❖ Cover and let stand at room temperature overnight.

❖ Bake at 350 degrees for 30 minutes.

❖ Yield: 6 servings

Approx Per Serving:
Cal 478; Prot 6 g; Carbo 66 g; T Fat 22 g;
41% Calories from Fat; Chol 32 mg;
Fiber 2 g; Sod 533 mg

Apple Streusel Coffee Cake

For the streusel, mix the brown sugar, 3/4 cup flour, butter and cinnamon in a medium bowl until the mixture is crumbly and the butter is completely incorporated. Stir in the walnuts.

❖ Mix 31/4 cups flour, baking powder and baking soda in a small bowl.

❖ Cream the margarine and sugar in a mixer bowl for 2 minutes or until light and fluffy. Beat in the eggs 1 at a time. Beat in the vanilla and yogurt.

❖ Add the flour mixture gradually, beating at low speed just until blended and scraping the bowl as needed.

❖ Spread 3 cups of the batter in a greased nonstick bundt pan. Sprinkle with 3/4 cup of the streusel. Add the apples and sprinkle with 1/2 cup of the streusel. Spread with the remaining batter. Sprinkle with the remaining streusel, pressing down lightly so that it sticks to the batter.

❖ Bake at 350 degrees for 50 to 60 minutes or until a wooden pick inserted near the center comes out clean. Cool in the pan on a wire rack for 15 minutes. Place a baking sheet over the pan and carefully invert both. Remove the pan and cool completely.

❖ Invert onto a serving plate.

❖ Yield: 16 servings

Approx Per Serving:
Cal 450; Prot 7 g; Carbo 61 g; T Fat 21 g; 41% Calories from Fat; Chol 57 mg; Fiber 2 g; Sod 269 mg

Janice M. Warren

11/4 cups packed brown sugar
3/4 cup flour
1/2 cup cold butter, cut into small pieces
2 teaspoons cinnamon
1 cup coarsely chopped walnuts
31/4 cups flour
11/2 teaspoons baking powder
3/4 teaspoon baking soda
3/4 cup margarine, at room temperature
11/4 cups sugar
3 eggs
2 teaspoons vanilla extract
2 cups low-fat yogurt
2 to 3 apples, sliced

119

Robbie's Coffee Cake

Robbie Timmons

News Anchor at WXYZ TV, Channel 7.

2 cups flour
1 1/2 teaspoons baking
    powder
1 teaspoon baking soda
1/2 cup melted butter,
    cooled
1 cup sugar
2 eggs
1 cup sour cream
1 teaspoon vanilla extract
1 cup chopped pecans or
    walnuts
1/2 cup sugar
1 teaspoon cinnamon

Mix the flour, baking powder and baking soda together.

❖ Combine the butter, 1 cup sugar, eggs, sour cream and vanilla in a large bowl and blend well. Add the flour mixture gradually, mixing well after each addition. Pour into a nonstick 8- or 9-inch baking pan.

❖ Mix the pecans, 1/2 cup sugar and cinnamon in a small bowl. Swirl through the batter.

❖ Bake at 350 degrees for 1 hour.

❖ Yield: 9 servings

Approx Per Serving:
Cal 481; Prot 6 g; Carbo 58 g; T Fat 26 g; 48% Calories from Fat; Chol 86 mg; Fiber 2 g; Sod 279 mg

120

Cinnamon Coffee Cake

Mix the flour, baking powder, baking soda and salt together.

❖ Cream the butter and 2 cups sugar in a mixer bowl until light and fluffy. Add the vanilla. Beat in the eggs 1 at a time.

❖ Add the flour mixture and sour cream alternately, beating just enough to keep the batter smooth after each addition.

❖ Spoon 1/3 of the batter into a greased tube pan. Mix the cinnamon, walnuts and 3/4 cup sugar in a small bowl. Sprinkle 1/3 of the mixture over the batter. Repeat the layers twice.

❖ Bake at 350 degrees for 1 hour and 10 minutes.

❖ Cool in the pan for 10 minutes. Remove to a wire rack to cool completely.

❖ Yield: 20 servings

Approx Per Serving:
Cal 342; Prot 4 g; Carbo 44 g; T Fat 17 g;
44% Calories from Fat; Chol 78 mg;
Fiber 1 g; Sod 300 mg

Sara Hickey

3 cups flour
2 teaspoons baking powder
1 teaspoon baking soda
1 teaspoon salt
1 cup butter or margarine, softened
2 cups sugar
2 teaspoons vanilla extract
4 eggs
2 cups sour cream
2 tablespoons ground cinnamon
1/2 cup chopped walnuts
3/4 cup sugar

121

Grandma's Coffee Cake

Virginia Simson Nelson

1 1/2 cups flour
2 teaspoons baking
   powder
3/4 to 1 cup sugar
3 tablespoons melted
   butter or margarine
1 teaspoon vanilla extract
1 egg
3/4 cup milk
1 cup fresh blueberries
1/2 cup sugar
1 teaspoon cinnamon

Mix the flour, baking powder, 3/4 to 1 cup sugar, butter, vanilla, egg and milk in a bowl. Pour into a greased 9- or 10-inch round baking pan.

❖ Top with the blueberries and a mixture of 1/2 cup sugar and cinnamon.

❖ Bake at 350 degrees for 20 to 25 minutes or until the coffee cake tests done.

❖ Yield: 8 servings

Approx Per Serving:
Cal 303; Prot 4 g; Carbo 59 g; T Fat 6 g;
18% Calories from Fat; Chol 41 mg;
Fiber 1 g; Sod 147 mg

Irish Soda Bread

Deborah C. Sullivan

2 cups flour
1/2 cup sugar
1/2 teaspoon each baking
   soda, baking powder
   and salt
1/4 cup butter
1 cup raisins
1 egg
2/3 cup buttermilk

Combine the first 5 ingredients in a large bowl and mix well. Cut in the butter until crumbly. Stir in the raisins.

❖ Beat the egg in a measuring cup. Add enough buttermilk to measure 1 cup. Add to the flour mixture, stirring until the dough leaves the side of the bowl.

❖ Turn onto a floured surface. Knead for 3 to 4 minutes or until smooth. Shape into an 8-inch circle. Mark with a cross. Place in a greased 8-inch baking pan.

❖ Bake at 375 degrees for 35 to 40 minutes or until the bread tests done.

❖ Yield: 8 servings

Approx Per Serving:
Cal 293; Prot 5 g; Carbo 54 g; T Fat 7 g;
21% Calories from Fat; Chol 43 mg;
Fiber 2 g; Sod 296 mg

Brunch, Bread & Beverages

Yorkshire Pudding

Michele has been the Assistant Director of several television shows produced in Hollywood.

Mix the flour and salt in a small mixer bowl. Add the milk gradually, beating well after each addition. Add the water and eggs. Beat until the mixture is bubbly. Let stand, covered, in a cool place for 30 minutes; do not refrigerate.

❖ Preheat the oven to 500 degrees. Pour the roast beef drippings into a 9x13-inch baking pan. Heat for 2 minutes.

❖ Beat the batter until bubbles form. Pour into the heated pan.

❖ Bake for 10 minutes. Reduce the oven temperature to 450 degrees.

❖ Bake for 12 to 15 minutes longer or until browned and crisp. Cut into squares and serve immediately.

❖ Yield: 8 servings

Approx Per Serving:
Cal 98; Prot 3 g; Carbo 6 g; T Fat 7 g;
62% Calories from Fat; Chol 60 mg;
Fiber <1 g; Sod 157 mg

Michele Capparelli-Lally

1/2 cup sifted flour
1/2 teaspoon salt
1/2 cup milk
1/4 cup cold water
2 eggs, lightly beaten
3 tablespoons roast beef
   drippings

123

Brunch, Bread & Beverages

Holden Christmas Punch

Barbara Lanese, RN

1 (46-ounce) can
  pineapple juice
4 (6-ounce) cans frozen
  limeade concentrate
2 quarts lemon-lime soda
1 fifth of vodka
1 pint frozen strawberries

Mix the pineapple juice, limeade concentrate, soda and vodka in a punch bowl. Stir in the strawberries.

❖ Garnish with an ice ring.

❖ Yield: 30 servings

Approx Per Serving:
Cal 152; Prot <1 g; Carbo 25 g; T Fat <1 g;
<1% Calories from Fat; Chol 0 mg;
Fiber <1 g; Sod 8 mg

Hot Chocolate Mix

Diane Shember

1 (20-quart) package dry
  milk
1 (16-ounce) package
  chocolate drink mix
1 (16-ounce) jar chocolate
  malted
1 (16-ounce) jar
  powdered nondairy
  coffee creamer
2 tablespoons (heaping)
  cinnamon
2 tablespoons (heaping)
  baking cocoa, sifted

Combine the dry milk, drink mix, chocolate malted, coffee creamer, cinnamon and cocoa in a large container and mix well. Store in an airtight container.

❖ Fill mugs 1/2 full with the mix. Fill with boiling water and mix well.

❖ Yield: 80 servings

Approx Per Serving:
Cal 209; Prot 14 g; Carbo 32 g; T Fat 3 g;
12% Calories from Fat; Chol 8 mg;
Fiber 1 g; Sod 256 mg

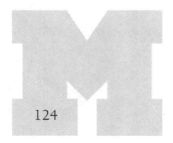

124

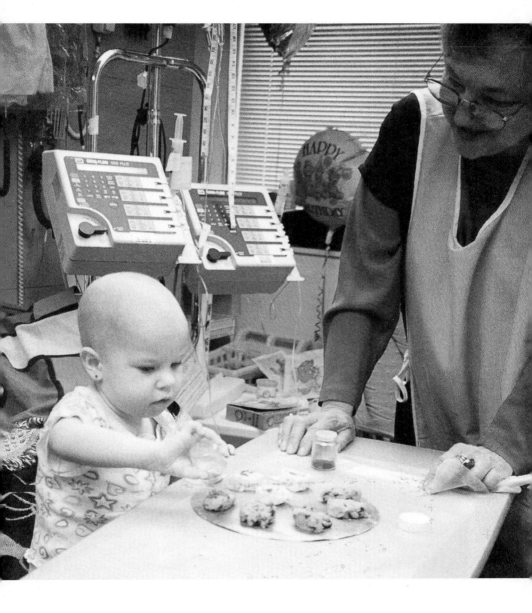

Desserts

C. S. Mott Children's Hospital

Ed and Julie Jonna

Ed and Julie Jonna from the Merchant of Vino have donated hours of their time and thousands of dollars in gifts in kind to a variety of our fundraisers. We appreciate their generous support of C. S. Mott Children's Hospital.

Rhubarb Raspberry Crisp

Combine the rhubarb, sugar, orange zest and orange juice in a large bowl and mix well.

❖ Mix the flour, brown sugar and cinnamon in a medium bowl. Rub in the butter until large crumbs form. Stir in the oats.

❖ Spoon the rhubarb mixture into a 1¹/₂-quart baking dish. Scatter the raspberries evenly over the mixture. Cover with the flour mixture.

❖ Bake at 350 degrees for 45 minutes or until the topping is browned and crisp and the mixture is bubbly. Let cool slightly before serving.

❖ May add ¹/₄ cup chopped toasted hazelnuts to the flour mixture.

❖ Yield: 10 servings

Approx Per Serving:
Cal 253; Prot 3 g; Carbo 40 g; T Fat 10 g;
34% Calories from Fat; Chol 25 mg;
Fiber 3 g; Sod 8 mg

Juliette Jonna

1¹/₂ pounds rhubarb, cut
    into 1-inch pieces
²/₃ cup sugar
Grated zest and juice of 1
    orange
1 cup flour
¹/₂ cup packed dark
    brown sugar
¹/₂ teaspoon cinnamon
¹/₂ cup cold unsalted
    butter, cut into small
    pieces
¹/₂ cup rolled oats
¹/₂ pint fresh raspberries

Desserts

Desserts

Apple Cake Dessert

Mix the flour, baking soda, salt and cinnamon in a large bowl.

❖ Mix the oil and sugar in a medium bowl. Add the eggs, mixing to blend. Add to the flour mixture and mix well. Stir in the flavorings. Add the apples and pecans and mix well. Pour into a 9x13-inch glass baking dish.

❖ Bake at 275 degrees for 1 hour and 20 minutes.

❖ Drizzle a mixture of the confectioners' sugar and lemon juice over the warm dessert.

❖ Yield: 15 servings

Approx Per Serving:
Cal 501; Prot 4 g; Carbo 59 g; T Fat 29 g;
52% Calories from Fat; Chol 43 mg;
Fiber 2 g; Sod 212 mg

Diane Shember

3 cups flour
1 teaspoon baking soda
1 teaspoon salt
1 teaspoon cinnamon
1 1/2 cups vegetable oil
2 cups sugar
3 eggs, beaten
1 teaspoon vanilla extract
1 teaspoon lemon extract
3 cups sliced tart apples
1 cup chopped pecans
1 cup confectioners' sugar
Juice of 2 lemons

Legal Brownies

Edward Goldman

4 eggs
2 cups sugar
4 ounces unsweetened
    chocolate, melted
2/3 cup melted margarine
2 teaspoons vanilla
    extract
1 1/3 cups flour
1 teaspoon baking
    powder
1/2 teaspoon salt
1 cup semisweet
    chocolate chips

Beat the eggs in a bowl. Beat in the sugar. Stir in the chocolate, margarine and vanilla. Add the flour, baking powder and salt, stirring just until mixed. Stir in the chocolate chips. Pour into a greased 9x13-inch baking pan.

❖ Bake at 350 degrees for 30 minutes or until the brownies test done.

❖ Cut into bars.

❖ Yield: 35 servings

Approx Per Serving:
Cal 141; Prot 2 g; Carbo 19 g; T Fat 7 g;
44% Calories from Fat; Chol 24 mg;
Fiber 1 g; Sod 89 mg

130

Desserts

P lace 24 foil cupcake liners on a baking sheet.

❖ Combine the brownie mix, egg, water and oil in a large bowl and mix well. Stir in the walnuts if packaged separately. Spoon 2 heaping tablespoonfuls of batter into each cupcake liner.

❖ Bake at 350 degrees for 20 to 25 minutes or until the brownies test done. Remove the liners and invert the brownies onto a wire rack to cool.

❖ Blend the confectioners' sugar and milk in a bowl. Spoon over 1 brownie at a time, spreading to cover completely. Top with the walnut halves. Let the glaze set.

❖ Place the chocolate chips and shortening in a sealable plastic bag. Seal and place in a bowl of hot water; let stand for several minutes. Knead until blended. Snip a pinpoint hole in a corner of the bag. Drizzle over the brownies.

❖ Store in an airtight container.

❖ Yield: 24 servings

Approx Per Serving:
Cal 262; Prot 2 g; Carbo 44 g; T Fat 10 g;
32% Calories from Fat; Chol 10 mg;
Fiber 1 g; Sod 85 mg

Cathy Schembechler

1 (22-ounce) package
    brownie mix with
    walnuts
1 egg
1/3 cup water
1/3 cup vegetable oil
4 1/2 cups confectioners'
    sugar
1/2 cup milk
24 walnut halves
1/3 cup semisweet
    chocolate chips
1 tablespoon shortening

Chinese Chew

Kathleen McCormick Schulz

1/2 cup butter
1/2 cup flour
1/2 cup packed brown
    sugar
2 eggs
1 cup packed brown
    sugar
1 teaspoon vanilla extract
1 teaspoon salt
2 tablespoons flour
1 teaspoon baking
    powder
1 cup shredded coconut
1 cup chopped walnuts

Combine the butter, 1/2 cup flour and 1/2 cup brown sugar in a bowl and mix well. Pat into a greased 9x9-inch baking pan.

❖ Bake at 360 degrees for 18 minutes.

❖ Combine the eggs, 1 cup brown sugar, vanilla, salt, 2 tablespoons flour, baking powder, coconut and walnuts in a bowl and mix well. Pour over the baked layer.

❖ Bake at 360 degrees for 25 minutes.

❖ Yield: 9 servings

Approx Per Serving:
Cal 390; Prot 5 g; Carbo 44 g; T Fat 23 g;
52% Calories from Fat; Chol 75 mg;
Fiber 2 g; Sod 432 mg

Desserts

Bread Pudding

Beat the eggs in a medium bowl. Add the sugar, milk, nutmeg and cinnamon and mix well. Stir in the vanilla.

❖ Pour over the bread in a large bowl. Add the raisins and banana and mix well. Pour into a buttered casserole.

❖ Bake at 350 degrees for 20 to 25 minutes or until lightly browned.

❖ Yield: 6 servings

Approx Per Serving:
Cal 329; Prot 8 g; Carbo 65 g; T Fat 5 g;
14% Calories from Fat; Chol 80 mg;
Fiber 2 g; Sod 244 mg

Robbie Timmons

2 eggs
$2/3$ cup sugar
$1^1/2$ cups milk
$1/4$ teaspoon nutmeg
$1/4$ teaspoon cinnamon
1 teaspoon vanilla extract
7 to 8 slices bread, torn
    into small pieces
$3/4$ cup raisins
1 banana, sliced

133

Desserts

Easy Cheesecake

Trudy Widner

16 ounces cream cheese,
   softened
1 teaspoon lime or lemon
   juice
3/4 cup sugar
1/2 teaspoon vanilla
   extract
1 egg yolk
2 (8-count) cans crescent
   rolls
1 egg white

Combine the cream cheese, lime juice, sugar, vanilla and egg yolk in a mixer bowl. Beat until blended.

❖ Unroll the crescent roll dough. Spread 1 package of the roll dough in a greased 9x12-inch baking pan, pressing to seal the perforations. Spread with the cream cheese mixture. Cover with the remaining dough. Brush with the egg white.

❖ Bake at 350 degrees for 25 minutes.

❖ Cut into squares. Store leftovers in the refrigerator.

❖ May dust with confectioners' sugar after baking.

❖ Yield: 12 servings

Approx Per Serving:
Cal 300; Prot 5 g; Carbo 31 g; T Fat 18 g;
52% Calories from Fat; Chol 63 mg;
Fiber <1 g; Sod 450 mg

134

Desserts

Whiffletree White Chocolate Mousse

Mix the vanilla wafers and butter in a bowl. Press over the bottom of a springform pan.

❖ Melt the chocolate in a double boiler over simmering water. Let cool to 95 degrees on a candy thermometer.

❖ Beat the egg whites at medium speed in a mixer bowl until stiff but not dry. Beat the whipping cream at medium speed in a mixer bowl until stiff peaks form.

❖ Beat the chocolate in a mixer bowl. Add the eggs, egg yolks and crème de cacao and beat until smooth. Add a small amount of the egg whites and whipping cream. Beat for 15 seconds. Fold in the remaining egg whites and whipping cream. Pour into the springform pan. Cover with plastic wrap and freeze overnight.

❖ Let stand for several minutes before serving. Press the raspberries through a sieve. Spread the raspberries over the dessert.

❖ Yield: 12 servings

Approx Per Serving:
Cal 589; Prot 8 g; Carbo 52 g; T Fat 40 g;
60% Calories from Fat; Chol 202 mg;
Fiber 2 g; Sod 227 mg

Rosanne Whitehouse

3 cups chopped vanilla
    wafers
1/2 cup melted butter
1 pound white chocolate
4 egg whites
2 cups whipping cream
2 eggs
4 egg yolks
2 tablespoons white
    crème de cacao
1 (16-ounce) package
    frozen raspberries

135

Desserts

Pineapple Dream Cake

Edna Miller

1 (1-layer) package white or yellow cake mix
1 (4-ounce) package vanilla, French vanilla or pineapple instant pudding mix
2 cups milk
8 ounces cream cheese, softened
1 (20-ounce) can crushed pineapple, drained
8 ounces whipped topping

Prepare the cake mix using the package directions. Pour into a nonstick 9x13-inch cake pan.

❖ Bake at 350 degrees until the layer tests done.

❖ Beat the pudding mix with the milk in a mixer bowl until the mixture begins to thicken. Add the cream cheese and mix well. Pour over the baked layer. Sprinkle the pineapple over the top. Spread with the whipped topping.

❖ Chill for several hours to overnight.

❖ Yield: 15 servings

Approx Per Serving:
Cal 333; Prot 5 g; Carbo 47 g; T Fat 15 g;
39% Calories from Fat; Chol 21 mg;
Fiber 1 g; Sod 428 mg

136

Desserts

Rhubarb Cheese Torte

Combine the rhubarb, 2/3 cup sugar and Triple Sec in a saucepan. Bring to a boil over medium heat, stirring occasionally; reduce the heat. Simmer for 15 minutes or until the mixture is thickened and the rhubarb is tender. Set aside to cool.

❖ Combine the flour, 1/2 cup sugar, walnuts, cinnamon and orange zest in a food processor container. Process until the walnuts are finely chopped. Add the butter. Process just until crumbly. Press half the mixture over the bottom of a buttered 9-inch springform pan. Reserve the remaining crumb mixture.

❖ Combine the ricotta cheese, cream cheese and 1/2 cup sugar in a mixer bowl. Beat until smooth. Beat in the vanilla. Beat in the eggs 1 at a time.

❖ Pour the rhubarb mixture into the prepared springform pan. Top with the cheese mixture, spreading evenly with a spatula.

❖ Bake at 350 degrees for 40 minutes. Sprinkle with the reserved crumb mixture. Bake for 20 minutes longer or until golden brown.

❖ Cool completely on a wire rack. Chill for several hours. Remove the side of the pan. Cut into generous wedges.

❖ Yield: 8 servings

Approx Per Serving:
Cal 627; Prot 14 g; Carbo 63 g; T Fat 35 g; 49% Calories from Fat; Chol 169 mg; Fiber 2 g; Sod 158 mg

Rob Jones

4 cups chopped fresh rhubarb
2/3 cup sugar
1/3 cup Triple Sec or other orange liqueur
1 cup unbleached flour
1/2 cup sugar
1/2 cup walnut pieces
2 teaspoons ground cinnamon
1 tablespoon grated orange zest
1/2 cup unsalted butter, softened, cut into small pieces
15 ounces ricotta cheese
8 ounces cream cheese, softened
1/2 cup sugar
2 teaspoons vanilla extract
3 eggs

137

Desserts

Sugarplum Pudding

Robbie Timmons

2 cups flour
2 1/2 teaspoons baking
   powder
1/2 teaspoon salt
2 1/2 cups sugar
1 1/4 teaspoons baking
   soda
1 teaspoon each allspice,
   cinnamon and nutmeg
3/4 cup vegetable oil
3 eggs
1 1/2 cups buttermilk
1 cup chopped prunes
1 cup chopped walnuts
1/2 cup margarine
1 teaspoon vanilla extract
1 tablespoon corn syrup

Combine the flour, baking powder, salt, 1 1/2 cups of the sugar, baking soda, allspice, cinnamon and nutmeg in a large bowl and mix well. Add the oil, eggs, 1 cup of the buttermilk, prunes and walnuts and mix well. Pour into 2 or 3 greased and floured 4x7-inch baking pans or molds.

❖ Bake at 325 degrees for 50 minutes; the mixture will rise 2 1/2 inches during baking.

❖ Combine the margarine, vanilla, 1/2 cup buttermilk, light corn syrup and 1 cup sugar in a small saucepan. Bring to a boil. Simmer until the margarine is melted, stirring frequently.

❖ Pour most of the glaze over the pudding in the pans, pulling the pudding away from the sides of the pans to allow the glaze to run down. Invert onto plates and remove the pans. Pour the remaining glaze over the pudding.

❖ Store in the refrigerator.

❖ Yield: 24 servings

Approx Per Serving:
Cal 296; Prot 3 g; Carbo 40 g; T Fat 15 g; 43% Calories from Fat; Chol 27 mg; Fiber 2 g; Sod 193 mg

138

Grandma's Suet Pudding

Combine the currants, suet, flour, raisins, sugar, salt and cinnamon in a bowl and mix well. Add 1 to 1¹/₂ cups milk gradually, beating until the batter forms a stiff paste. Pour into a metal mold.

❖ Steam over boiling water for 2¹/₂ hours.

❖ Thin the cornstarch with 1 teaspoon milk. Combine with the butter and sugar in a saucepan. Heat until the butter is melted, stirring constantly. Add enough hot milk to thicken to a sauce consistency.

❖ Serve the warm sauce over the warm pudding.

❖ Yield: 6 servings

Approx Per Serving:
Cal 836; Prot 9 g; Carbo 113 g; T Fat 41 g;
43% Calories from Fat; Chol 40 mg;
Fiber 4 g; Sod 106 mg

Judi Stanford

1 cup currants
1 cup ground suet
2 cups flour
1 cup raisins
1 cup sugar
¹/₈ teaspoon salt
1 teaspoon cinnamon
1 to 1¹/₂ cups milk
1 tablespoon cornstarch
1 teaspoon milk
1 tablespoon butter
2 tablespoons sugar
¹/₄ cup hot milk

139

Desserts

Welsh Cakes

Susan John

3 cups flour
1 1/2 cups sugar
1 tablespoon baking
   powder
1 teaspoon nutmeg
1 teaspoon cinnamon
1 cup raisins, currants or
   dried tart cherries
1 cup lard, shortening or
   margarine
1 egg, or equivalent egg
   substitute
2/3 cup milk

Sift the flour, sugar, baking powder, nutmeg and cinnamon together. Stir in the raisins and lard. Add the egg and milk and mix until a firm dough forms.

❖ Roll 1/4 inch thick on a lightly floured surface. Cut into 3- to 4-inch rounds.

❖ Bake on a nonstick skillet or griddle over low heat until golden brown, turning once.

❖ Yield: 30 servings

Approx Per Serving:
Cal 169; Prot 2 g; Carbo 24 g; T Fat 7 g;
39% Calories from Fat; Chol 14 mg;
Fiber 1 g; Sod 39 mg

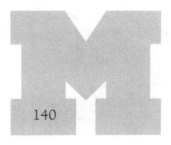

Desserts

Shari's Choco-Cinnamon Cookies

Combine the flour, baking soda, salt and cinnamon in a bowl and mix well.

❖ Beat the butter and margarine in a mixer bowl. Add the sugar and brown sugar and mix well. Beat in the eggs and vanilla. Add the flour mixture 1/3 at a time, beating well after each addition. Stir in the chocolate.

❖ Drop by 1-inch scoopfuls onto a nonstick 12x15-inch cookie sheet.

❖ Bake at 375 degrees for 11 minutes or until golden brown.

❖ Yield: 40 servings

Approx Per Serving:
Cal 153; Prot 2 g; Carbo 20 g; T Fat 8 g;
46% Calories from Fat; Chol 17 mg;
Fiber 1 g; Sod 130 mg

Shari L. Hartley

2 1/4 cups flour, sifted
1 teaspoon baking soda
1 teaspoon salt
1/4 cup ground cinnamon
1/2 cup butter, softened
1/2 cup margarine, softened
3/4 cup sugar
3/4 cup packed light brown sugar
2 eggs
1 teaspoon vanilla extract
1 (16-ounce) package semisweet chocolate chunks

141

Crispy Chocolate Chip Cookies

Therese Wion

1 teaspoon baking soda
1 tablespoon milk
1 cup vegetable oil
1 cup shortening
1 egg
1 cup sugar
1 cup packed brown
    sugar
1/2 teaspoon salt
1 teaspoon cream of tartar
1 cup rolled oats
3 cups flour
1 1/2 cups crisp rice cereal
1 cup chocolate chips

Dissolve the baking soda in the milk. Combine with the oil, shortening and egg in a bowl and mix well.

❖ Add the sugar, brown sugar, salt, cream of tartar, oats and flour and mix well. Stir in the cereal and chocolate chips.

❖ Shape into 1-inch balls. Place on a nonstick cookie sheet.

❖ Bake at 325 degrees for 15 to 20 minutes or until crispy and browned.

❖ May add 1 cup chopped pecans or walnuts with the cereal.

❖ Yield: 24 servings

Approx Per Serving:
Cal 331; Prot 3 g; Carbo 36 g; T Fat 20 g; 54% Calories from Fat; Chol 9 mg; Fiber 1 g; Sod 107 mg

142

Desserts

Hazelnut Biscotti

Mix the flour, baking powder, ginger and salt together.

❖ Cream the butter and sugar in a mixer bowl. Add the vanilla, egg and orange peel, beating until light and fluffy. Add the flour mixture gradually, beating well after each addition. Stir in the hazelnuts.

❖ Shape into two 2x12-inch logs on a cookie sheet lined with waxed paper. Bake at 350 degrees for 15 minutes or until browned. Cool for 10 minutes on a wire rack.

❖ Reduce the oven temperature to 300 degrees. Cut the biscotti logs diagonally into 1/4-inch slices. Return to the cookie sheet. Bake for 20 minutes or until toasted, turning once.

❖ Let stand to dry completely before storing in an airtight container.

❖ May substitute 1 cup chopped roasted almonds for the hazelnuts, 2 teaspoons grated lemon peel for the orange peel and 1 teaspoon anise seeds for the vanilla.

❖ Yield: 48 servings

Approx Per Serving:
Cal 59; Prot 1 g; Carbo 6 g; T Fat 4 g;
54% Calories from Fat; Chol 10 mg;
Fiber <1 g; Sod 54 mg

Tonie Leeds

1 1/4 cups flour
1 1/2 teaspoons baking
  powder
1/8 teaspoon ground
  ginger
1/2 teaspoon salt
1/2 cup butter, softened
3/4 cup sugar
1 teaspoon vanilla extract
1 large egg, or 2 small
  eggs
2 teaspoons grated orange
  peel
1 cup chopped roasted
  hazelnuts

143

Desserts

Forgotten Cookies

Kathleen McCormick Schulz

2 egg whites
2/3 cup sugar
1 cup chocolate chips
1 cup walnut pieces

Beat the egg whites in a mixer bowl until stiff peaks form. Add the sugar, beating constantly until the mixture is shiny.

❖ Fold in the chocolate chips and walnuts.

❖ Drop by 1 large round spoonful onto a foil-lined cookie sheet. Place in a 350-degree oven. Turn off the oven. Let stand overnight.

❖ Yield: 20 servings

Approx Per Serving:
Cal 107; Prot 2 g; Carbo 13 g; T Fat 6 g;
49% Calories from Fat; Chol 0 mg;
Fiber 1 g; Sod 7 mg

144

Cream the margarine, sugar, brown sugar and eggs in a mixer bowl until light and fluffy.

❖ Add the vanilla, corn syrup, baking soda, peanut butter and oats and mix well. Stir in the chocolate chips and candy.

❖ Drop by large spoonfuls onto a nonstick cookie sheet.

❖ Bake at 350 degrees for 10 minutes or until golden brown.

❖ Yield: 100 servings

Approx Per Serving:
Cal 149; Prot 4 g; Carbo 18 g; T Fat 8 g;
44% Calories from Fat; Chol 13 mg;
Fiber 1 g; Sod 100 mg

Steve and Kate Lambright

1 cup margarine, softened
2 1/4 cups sugar
2 1/4 cups packed brown sugar
6 eggs
1/2 tablespoon vanilla extract
1/2 tablespoon corn syrup
4 teaspoons baking soda
3 cups chunky peanut butter
9 cups rolled oats
1 1/3 cups chocolate chips
8 ounces "M & M's" Chocolate Candies

145

Desserts

Scotch 100% Natural Cookies

Therese Wion

2 cups flour
2 teaspoons baking
    powder
1 teaspoon baking soda
1 teaspoon salt
3/4 cup sugar
3/4 cup packed brown
    sugar
1 cup melted butter
2 eggs
1 tablespoon water
1 1/2 cups 100% Natural
    Quaker Cereal
2 cups butterscotch chips

Mix the flour, baking powder, baking soda and salt together.

❖ Cream the sugar, brown sugar, butter, eggs and water in a mixer bowl until light and fluffy. Add the flour mixture gradually, beating well after each addition. Stir in the cereal and butterscotch chips.

❖ Drop by tablespoonfuls onto a greased cookie sheet.

❖ Bake at 375 degrees for 10 to 12 minutes or until golden brown.

❖ Yield: 24 servings

Approx Per Serving:
Cal 262; Prot 3 g; Carbo 33 g; T Fat 14 g; 46% Calories from Fat; Chol 39 mg; Fiber 1 g; Sod 252 mg

146

Combine the shortening, salt, cinnamon, molasses, sugar and egg in a mixer bowl and beat well. Add the flour and baking soda and beat well; the batter will be thick.

❖ Stir in the pecans, raisins, dates and oats. Drop by teaspoonfuls onto a greased cookie sheet.

❖ Bake at 350 degrees for 10 to 15 minutes or until lightly browned. The cookies will be soft at first; let cool slightly before removing from the cookie sheet.

❖ Serve with ice cream or chopped fresh fruit.

❖ Yield: 24 servings

Approx Per Serving:
Cal 129; Prot 2 g; Carbo 18 g; T Fat 6 g;
40% Calories from Fat; Chol 9 mg;
Fiber 1 g; Sod 118 mg

Patricia F. Waller

1/2 cup shortening or
    softened margarine
1 teaspoon salt
1 teaspoon cinnamon
1 teaspoon molasses
1 cup sugar
1 egg
1 cup sifted flour
3/4 teaspoon baking soda
1/3 cup chopped pecans
    or walnuts
1/3 cup raisins
1/3 cup chopped dates
1 cup rolled or quick-
    cooking oats

147

Desserts

Banana Chocolate Chip Cakes

Marylen S. Oberman

1/2 cup butter or
    margarine, softened
1²/₃ cups sugar
2 eggs, slightly beaten
1/4 teaspoon salt
1¹/₂ teaspoons baking
    powder
1¹/₂ teaspoons baking
    soda
1/4 cup nonfat yogurt or
    sour cream
1 cup mashed very ripe
    bananas
2 cups cake flour, or 1¹/₂
    cups all-purpose flour
1 teaspoon vanilla extract
1 to 2 cups chocolate
    chips

Cream the butter and sugar in a mixer bowl until light and fluffy. Add the eggs and salt and mix well.

❖ Dissolve the baking powder and baking soda in the yogurt. Add to the creamed mixture and mix well. Stir in the bananas.

❖ Add the flour gradually, mixing well after each addition. Stir in the vanilla and chocolate chips.

❖ Pour into two 5x9-inch or 4 miniature loaf pans sprayed with nonstick cooking spray. Bake at 350 degrees for 1¹/₂ hours.

❖ Freezes well. Thaw slightly before serving.

❖ Recipe may be doubled; use 4 very ripe bananas and 1/2 to 1 cup chocolate chips.

❖ Yield: 24 servings

Approx Per Serving:
Cal 204; Prot 2 g; Carbo 31 g; T Fat 10 g;
40% Calories from Fat; Chol 28 mg;
Fiber 1 g; Sod 172 mg

148

Double Chocolate Bundt Cake

Combine the cake mix, 2/3 cup water, eggs and sour cream in a large mixer bowl. Beat at low speed until moistened.

❖ Fold in the chocolate chips. Pour into a greased and floured bundt pan.

❖ Bake at 350 degrees for 40 to 45 minutes or until the cake springs back when lightly touched. Cool in the pan for 10 minutes. Invert onto a wire rack or serving plate to cool completely.

❖ Combine the frosting and 2 teaspoons water in a bowl. Mix until of a glaze consistency, adding a few more drops of water if needed. Drizzle over the cake.

❖ Yield: 12 servings

Approx Per Serving:
Cal 376; Prot 6 g; Carbo 54 g; T Fat 16 g;
38% Calories from Fat; Chol 62 mg;
Fiber 2 g; Sod 425 mg

Marilyn Hawkins

1 (2-layer) package pudding-recipe chocolate fudge, devil's food or sour cream chocolate cake mix
2/3 cup water
3 eggs
1 cup sour cream
1 cup miniature chocolate chips
1/2 cup prepared chocolate frosting
2 teaspoons (or more) water

149

Desserts

Peanut Butter Cake

Carl D. Ent

Chief of Police
Ann Arbor, Michigan

1¹/₂ cups flour
1 cup sugar
1 teaspoon baking soda
¹/₂ teaspoon salt
1 cup warm water
¹/₄ cup peanut butter
5 tablespoons melted
    butter
1 teaspoon vanilla extract
2 cups confectioners'
    sugar
¹/₃ cup melted butter
1¹/₂ tablespoons peanut
    butter
1¹/₂ teaspoons vanilla
    extract
¹/₄ cup milk

Combine the flour, sugar, baking soda, salt, warm water, ¹/₄ cup peanut butter, 5 tablespoons butter and 1 teaspoon vanilla in a bowl and mix well. Pour into a greased 8x8-inch or 9x9-inch cake pan.

❖ Bake at 350 degrees for 25 minutes.

❖ Combine the confectioners' sugar, ¹/₃ cup butter, 1¹/₂ tablespoons peanut butter and 1¹/₂ teaspoons vanilla in a bowl and mix well. Add the milk gradually, beating until of a spreading consistency.

❖ Spread over the cooled cake.

❖ Yield: 12 servings

Approx Per Serving:
Cal 336; Prot 4 g; Carbo 50 g; T Fat 14 g;
37% Calories from Fat; Chol 27 mg;
Fiber 1 g; Sod 296 mg

150

Poppy Seed Cake

Combine the cake mix, pudding mix, oil and poppy seeds in a mixer bowl and beat well.

❖ Add small amounts of the boiling water and the eggs alternately, mixing well after each addition and beating for 2 minutes after adding the last egg.

❖ Pour into a bundt pan sprayed with nonstick cooking spray. Bake at 350 degrees for 30 to 40 minutes or until the cake tests done.

❖ Cool in the pan for several minutes. Invert onto a serving plate to cool completely. Sprinkle with the confectioners' sugar.

❖ Yield: 16 servings

Approx Per Serving:
Cal 262; Prot 3 g; Carbo 33 g; T Fat 13 g;
44% Calories from Fat; Chol 54 mg;
Fiber 1 g; Sod 315 mg

Raechelle Seaik

1 (2-layer) package yellow
  cake mix
1 (4-ounce) package
  vanilla instant
  pudding mix
1/2 cup vegetable oil
1/3 cup poppy seeds
1 cup boiling water
4 eggs
2 to 4 tablespoons
  confectioners' sugar

151

Strawberry Cake

Donna Auer

1 (2-layer) package yellow
    or white cake mix
1 (3-ounce) package
    strawberry gelatin
3/4 cup vegetable oil
1 cup chopped pecans or
    walnuts
4 eggs
2 tablespoons flour
1 (10-ounce) package
    frozen sliced
    strawberries, thawed
1 cup whipping cream
1 tablespoon sugar

Combine the cake mix, gelatin, oil, pecans, eggs, flour and strawberries in a large mixer bowl. Beat at medium speed for 3 minutes. Pour into a greased 10-inch angel food or bundt cake pan.

❖ Bake at 350 degrees for 55 to 65 minutes or until a wooden pick inserted near the center comes out clean. Cool on a wire rack for 10 minutes. Invert onto a serving plate to cool completely.

❖ Beat the whipping cream with the sugar in a mixer bowl until stiff peaks form. Serve with the cake.

❖ May serve with vanilla ice cream.

❖ Yield: 12 servings

Approx Per Serving:
Cal 508; Prot 6 g; Carbo 46 g; T Fat 34 g;
60% Calories from Fat; Chol 99 mg;
Fiber 2 g; Sod 326 mg

152

Desserts

Backyard Lemon Pie

Famous Hollywood writer whose credits include Wild Wild West, Mission Impossible *and* Ironsides

Combine the egg whites, cream of tartar, salt and vanilla in a large mixer bowl. Beat until foamy. Add 1 cup confectioners' sugar gradually, beating constantly until stiff peaks form. Spread over the bottom and up the side of a greased 9-inch pie plate.

❖ Bake at 275 degrees for 1 hour or until dry and firm. Let stand to cool.

❖ Beat the eggs yolks, sugar, lemon juice and lemon peel in a mixer bowl. Pour into a double boiler. Cook over hot water until thickened, stirring frequently. Remove from the heat and let cool.

❖ Fold in half the whipped cream. Pour into the meringue crust. Chill for 2 hours or longer.

❖ Stir 1 tablespoon confectioners' sugar into the remaining whipped cream. Spread over the cold pie.

❖ Yield: 6 servings

Approx Per Serving:
Cal 338; Prot 5 g; Carbo 40 g; T Fat 18 g;
47% Calories from Fat; Chol 196 mg;
Fiber <1 g; Sod 146 mg

Max Hodge

(class of 1939)

4 egg whites, at room
    temperature
1/2 teaspoon cream of
    tartar
1/4 teaspoon salt
1/2 teaspoon vanilla
    extract
1 cup confectioners' sugar
4 egg yolks
1/2 cup sugar
Juice and grated peel of 1
    large lemon or 2
    medium lemons
2 cups whipped cream or
    whipped topping
1 tablespoon (heaping)
    confectioners' sugar

153

Desserts

Old-Fashioned Pie Crusts

Gordon and Joy Berenson

5 cups flour
3 tablespoons sugar
1/2 teaspoon baking
   powder
1 (1-pound) package lard
3 tablespoons vinegar
1 egg

Mix the flour, sugar and baking powder in a bowl. Cut in the lard.

❖ Combine the vinegar and egg in a 1-cup glass measure. Add enough water to measure 1 cup. Add to the flour mixture gradually, mixing well after each addition.

❖ Let stand until the flour mixture absorbs the moisture. Shape into a ball. Cover and chill until needed.

❖ Yield: 16 servings

Approx Per Serving:
Cal 412; Prot 4 g; Carbo 32 g; T Fat 29 g;
64% Calories from Fat; Chol 40 mg;
Fiber 1 g; Sod 15 mg

Pie Crust

Patricia A. Warner

1 1/2 cups flour
1/2 teaspoon baking
   powder
1/2 teaspoon salt
2/3 cup shortening
1/4 cup boiling water

Sift the flour, baking powder and salt together.

❖ Combine the shortening and boiling water in a bowl. Mix with a fork until smooth.

❖ Add the flour mixture gradually, mixing well after each addition until a soft dough forms. Shape into a ball and cool.

❖ Roll between 2 sheets of waxed paper.

❖ Yield: 8 servings

Approx Per Serving:
Cal 237; Prot 2 g; Carbo 18 g; T Fat 17 g;
66% Calories from Fat; Chol 0 mg;
Fiber 1 g; Sod 154 mg

154

WHEN THE RECIPE CALLS FOR . . . . **USE**

1/2 cup butter	.4 ounces
4 cups all-purpose flour	.1 pound
1 square chocolate	.1 ounce
1 cup semisweet chocolate chips	.6 ounces
4 cups marshmallows	.1 pound
2¹/4 cups packed brown sugar	.1 pound
4 cups confectioners' sugar	.1 pound
2 cups granulated sugar	.1 pound
1 cup fine dry bread crumbs	.4 to 5 slices
1 cup soft bread crumbs	.2 slices
1 cup fine cracker crumbs	.28 saltines
1 cup crushed cornflakes	.3 cups uncrushed
4 cups cooked macaroni	.8 ounces uncooked
3¹/2 cups cooked rice	.1 cup uncooked
1 cup shredded cheese	.4 ounces
1 cup cottage cheese	.8 ounces
1 cup sour cream	.8 ounces
1 cup whipped cream	.¹/2 cup heavy cream
²/3 cup evaporated milk	.1 small can
1²/3 cups evaporated milk	.1 (13-ounce) can
4 cups sliced or chopped apples	.4 medium
1 cup mashed bananas	.3 medium
2¹/2 cups shredded coconut	.8 ounces
4 cups cranberries	.1 pound
3 to 4 tablespoons lemon juice plus	
1 tablespoon grated lemon rind	.1 lemon
¹/3 cup orange juice plus	
2 teaspoons grated orange rind	.1 orange
3 cups raisins	.1 (15-ounce) package
4 cups chopped cooked chicken	.1 (5-pound) chicken
3 cups chopped cooked meat	.1 pound, cooked
2 cups cooked ground meat	.1 pound, cooked
1 cup chopped nuts	.4 ounces shelled
1 cup grated carrot	.1 large
8 ounces fresh mushrooms	.1 (4-ounce) can
1 cup chopped onion	.1 large
4 cups sliced or chopped potatoes	.4 medium

155

Charts

Nutritional Profile Guidelines

The editors have attempted to present these family recipes in a form that allows approximate nutritional values to be computed. Persons with dietary or health problems or whose diets require close monitoring should not rely solely on the nutritional information provided. They should consult their physicians or a registered dietitian for specific information.

Abbreviations for Nutritional Profile

Cal — Calories   Fiber — Dietary Fiber   Sod — Sodium
Prot — Protein   T Fat — Total Fat   g — grams
Carbo — Carbohydrates   Chol — Cholesterol   mg — milligrams

Nutritional information for these recipes is computed from information derived from many sources, including materials supplied by the United States Department of Agriculture, computer databanks, and journals in which the information is assumed to be in the public domain. However, many specialty items, new products, and processed foods may not be available from these sources or may vary from the average values used in these profiles. More information on new and/or specific products may be obtained by reading the nutrient labels. Unless otherwise specified, the nutritional profile of these recipes is based on all measurements being level.

❖ **Artificial sweeteners** vary in use and strength so should be used "to taste," using the recipe ingredients as a guideline. Sweeteners using aspartame (NutraSweet and Equal) should not be used as a sweetener in recipes involving prolonged heating, which reduces the sweet taste. For further information on the use of these sweeteners, refer to package.

❖ **Alcoholic ingredients** have been analyzed for the basic ingredients, although cooking causes the evaporation of alcohol, thus decreasing alcoholic content.

156

Charts

❖ **Buttermilk**, **sour cream**, and **yogurt** are the types that are available commercially.

❖ **Cake mixes** which are prepared using package directions include 3 eggs and 1/2 cup oil.

❖ **Chicken**, cooked for boning and chopping, has been roasted; this method yields the lowest caloric content.

❖ **Cottage cheese** is cream-style with 4.2% creaming mixture. Dry curd cottage cheese has no creaming mixture.

❖ **Eggs** are all large. To avoid raw eggs that may carry salmonella, as in eggnog or 6-week muffin batter, use an equivalent amount of commercial egg substitute.

❖ **Flour** is unsifted all-purpose flour.

❖ **Garnishes**, serving suggestions, and other optional additions and variations are not included in this profile.

❖ **Margarine** and **butter** are regular, not whipped or presoftened.

❖ **Milk** is whole milk, 3.5% butterfat. Lowfat milk is 1% butterfat. Evaporated milk is whole milk with 60% of the water removed.

❖ **Oil** is any type of vegetable cooking oil. **Shortening** is hydrogenated vegetable shortening.

❖ **Salt** and other ingredients to taste as noted in the ingredients have not been included in the nutritional profile.

❖ If a choice of ingredients has been given, the nutritional profile reflects the first option. If a choice of amounts has been given, the nutritional profile reflects the greater amount.

157

Charts

Food Safety

What we think is the flu can sometimes be caused by harmful bacteria that may be in food. Bacteria on food can grow and make you sick. You can't always see, smell or taste if food is contaminated with bacteria—so it's important to buy safe food and keep it safe when you get home.

These are some foods that bacteria like best: milk and other dairy products; eggs; meat; poultry and seafood. When buying, storing and preparing foods, it's important to use safe food handling practices. Here are some tips to follow:

At the Store:

❖ Buy cans and jars that look perfect. Don't buy dented, rusted cans or cans with bulging ends. Check the carton of eggs to see if any are broken or cracked.

❖ Keep dripping meat juices away from other foods. Put raw meat, poultry and seafood into plastic bags before they go into your cart.

❖ Pick up milk and other cold foods last. This gives food less time to warm up before you get home.

❖ Pick up hot chicken and other hot foods just before you go to the checkout lane. This will give hot food less time to cool off before you get home.

Storing Food:

❖ Return home as soon as you can after shopping for food. Put food into the refrigerator or freezer right away. Eggs always go in the refrigerator.

Preparing Food:

❖ Wash your hands with warm water and soap before and after you handle food. Wash anything that comes in contact with food, such as utensils, counters, equipment, etc. Use paper towels to wipe up cupboard spills, especially meat juices.

❖ If you use a dishcloth, use one that has been freshly laundered and dried in your dryer. Rinse with hot soapy water after each use and hang to dry. Change dishcloths frequently. A dirty dishcloth can add more bacteria than it removes.

158

Charts

❖ Rinse fresh fruits and vegetables under running water to wash away dirt. Do not use dish detergent or hand soap to wash fruits and vegetables.

❖ Keep raw meat, poultry, and seafood and their juices away from other foods. These foods can spread bacteria in your kitchen.

❖ Keep meat, poultry, and seafood cold while they thaw. Thaw them:

   ❖ In the refrigerator, 1 to 2 days before you will cook the food.

   ❖ In the microwave, use the "defrost" setting. Then cook the food right away.

❖ Cook raw meat, poultry, seafood, and eggs until they are done. Use an oven temperature of at least 325 degrees F. to destroy bacteria.

   ❖ Cook red meat, especially ground meat, until it looks brown insde and the juices look clear, not pink.

   ❖ Poke cooked chicken with a fork. The juices should look clear, not pink.

   ❖ Stick a fork into cooked fish. The fish should flake.

   ❖ Cook eggs until whites and yolks are firm, not runny.

Handling Leftovers:

❖ Store leftovers in the refrigerator or freezer as soon as you finish eating. If food is left out for 2 or more hours, bacteria can grow. Put leftovers in shallow dishes so they cool faster.

❖ Eat leftovers in the next two days.

❖ IF IN DOUBT, THROW IT OUT!

Source: Alice Henneman, M.S.R.D., Lancaster County Extension Educator and Julie Albrecht, Ph.D.R.D., Associate Professor, Extension Food Specialist, University of Nebraska. Adapted from: *Keep Your Food Safe*, FDA, 1991.

159

Charts

The Mott Seurat

Seurat

A shrunken hospital bedsheet, acrylic paint, and one hundred and sixty-one young artists combined to recreate one of the masterpieces of pointillism, George Seurat's "Sunday Afternoon at the Grande Jatte Park."

Seurat was a visionary, but he never could have foreseen that more than a century after his creation, the children at C. S. Mott Children's Hospital would use his painting and his technique as a perfect vehicle for their own artistic expression. The youngsters spent twelve weeks recreating the painting it took Seurat 31 months to produce.

As the painting developed, it traveled all over the hospital... the hematology-oncology clinic, intensive care, moderate care, and in every room of the bone marrow unit. Many of the artists painted while they were in their hospital beds.

The gamut of artists ranged from a thirty-two-month old leukemia patient to a young woman awaiting a heart transplant that she subsequently underwent. Two quadriplegics painted by holding paint brushes in their mouths. Another patient recovering from the amputation of several fingers painted with his foot. One youngster painted with weights attached to her hands to keep them steady, and a child who is blind conjured up visions of a hot, summer day to relate his work to the spectrum of colors. A cancer patient worked on the painting until the orderly came to wheel her to surgery, and she was back at work the next afternoon.

The only deviations from the original painting were the smaller canvas and the use of brighter colors. The painting hangs in the lobby of the Maternal/Child Health Center as a tribute to all the children who pass through the lobby.

Seurat

A Long History of Service to Children

The University of Michigan Medical Center has a long and proud history in pediatrics. In fact, many of the men and women who have gone on to become national leaders in the field began their careers here.

At the turn of the century, when pediatrics was just emerging as a medical specialty, the University of Michigan moved to the forefront of practice and research—pioneering new treatments and setting standards for other health professionals to follow. During the early 1900s, the University of Michigan Hospital established a separate children's ward, one of the first units of its kind in the country.

It was in the mid-1960s that the C. S. Mott Foundation, responding to a growing need for a separate children's hospital and realizing the opportunity to build on an already strong foundation, stepped forward with a $6.5 million gift. C. S. Mott Children's Hospital opened its doors in 1969.

Since that time, our expertise in pediatrics has expanded from primary care to include numerous tertiary care subspecialties, all supported by pace-setting research. These activities and resources have placed Mott among the top children's hospitals in the nation.

C. S. Mott Children's Hospital is licensed for 200 beds and currently staffs 196 with occupancy year-to-date of 72.1 percent. The hospital ranks 7th in the country in percentage of intensive care beds— 65 of 196 beds.

162

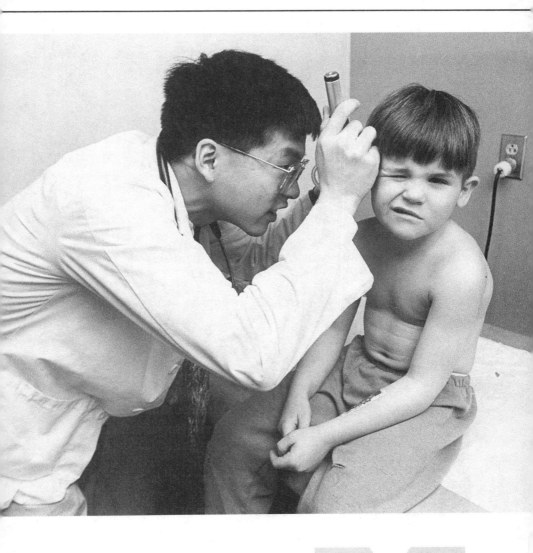

163

History

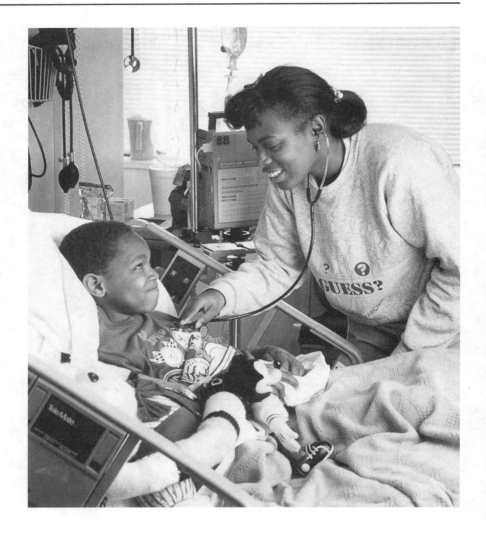

164

History

Specialists in Pediatric Care

In addition to providing expert primary care at Mott Children's Hospital, the hospital's outreach efforts extend to off-site clinics in the community and in clinics located throughout the state of Michigan. It helps young patients from around the world suffering from severe and complex heart problems by providing a full spectrum of cardiovascular care from pre-birth diagnoses to life-long follow-up. The Michigan Congential Heart Program is one of the largest and most highly regarded in the nation, devoted to caring for children of all ages.

Caring for children with a wide array of cancer-related problems, from blood disorders to tumors, is one of the hospital's specialty services. The hospital is a member of the national Childhood Cancer Group, a consortium of thirty major health centers nationwide with access to the newest and most effective treatments.

Children with neurological problems, from brain tumors to epilepsy, are cared for by an inter-disciplinary team that includes neuropsychologists, child neurol-ogists, nurses, social workers, and dieticians.

Young patients with recurring infections are cared for by a team of highly skilled pediatric infectious disease specialists. Children experiencing acute problems with genetic diseases, diabetes, hypertension, and other disorders involving the kidneys receive a wide range of care through the hospital's nephrology program.

The pediatric surgical services began in 1974 and they have earned a national reputation for outstanding care and leadership in such areas as head and neck disorders, major trauma, orthopaedics, urology, thoracic, abdominal, and vascular surgery. More than 6,500 pediatric surgical procedures are performed each year.

Mott Children's Hospital offers pediatric patients one of the broadest-based mental health treatment programs in the United States, both inpatient care and outpatient services, with special attention on adolescent mental health care.

Each year, more than 800 babies are admitted to the neonatal intensive care unit to receive therapy not routinely available at other hospitals.

165

Pediatric Care

Specialists in Pediatric Care

More than 7,000 young patients from throughout Michigan and neighboring states are cared for by the hospital's pediatric ophthalmologists and its team of specialists who diagnose and treat all aspects of sight problems in children.

The Pediatric Intensive Care unit has earned an international reputation for excellence in the care of children with respiratory failure.

Pediatric physical medicine specialists help young patients overcome problems related to head injuries, stroke, spinal cord injuries, cerebral palsy, and communications disorders and they conduct annual summer camps for children who use ventilators.

The hospital was a pioneer in the early 1980s in the development of ECMO (Extra Corporeal Membrane Oxygenation), which is a means of providing mechanical support for infants requiring temporary heart and lung assistance.

The Trauma Center treats approximately 500 young patients annually from throughout Michigan and the Midwest, many of whom are brought to the hospital by the Medical Center's Survival Flight helicopter.

Throughout all of this care, the focus is on the patient and family. Special facilities are provided for the convenience of the family and their visits to comfort young patients and assist in their recovery.

166

Pediatric Care

The University of Michigan Health System

University of Michigan Health System

1522 Simpson Road East
Ann Arbor, Michigan 48109-0718
(313) 936-9836

C. S. Mott Children's Hospital Administration

Patricia A. Warner, M.P.H., *administrator*
Jean E. Robillard, M.D., *physician-in-chief*
Arnold J. Coran, M.D., *surgeon-in-chief*
Carol D. Spengler, Ph.D., R.N., *director of patient care services*
Stephen A. Gaucher, *senior development officer*

Executive Officers of the Medical Center

Larry Warren, *interim executive director,*
  University of Michigan Health System
A. Lorris Betz, M.D., *interim dean, University of Michigan Medical School*

The Regents of the University

Deane Baker, Laurence B. Deitch,
Daniel D. Horning, Shirley M. McFee,
Rebecca McGowan, Andrea Fischer Newman,
Philip H. Power, Nellie M. Varner,
Homer A. Neal, *interim president (ex-officio)*

The University of Michigan is an equal opportunity/affirmative action employer.

The University of Michigan Health System is committed to Total Quality.

*C. S. Mott Children's Hospital is a member of NACHRI–
the National Association of Children's Hospitals and Related Institutions–
based in Washington, D.C.*

Index

168

Index

170

Index

Index

171

Index

Index

Index

Cookbook Order Form

Please send me _____ copy/copies of **Michigan Cooks.** (Books are $16.95 each; add $3.00 per book for postage.) Make checks payable to C. S. Mott Children's Hospital.

Name: _____

Street Address: _____

City _____ State: _____ Zip: _____

Mail to:
Michigan Cooks
Attention: Stephen A. Gaucher
C. S. Mott Children's Hospital
D5232 Medical Professional Bldg.
Ann Arbor, Michigan 48109-0718

Please send me _____ copy/copies of **Michigan Cooks.** (Books are $16.95 each; add $3.00 per book for postage.) Make checks payable to C. S. Mott Children's Hospital.

Name: _____

Street Address: _____

City _____ State: _____ Zip: _____

Mail to:
Michigan Cooks
Attention: Stephen A. Gaucher
C. S. Mott Children's Hospital
D5232 Medical Professional Bldg.
Ann Arbor, Michigan 48109-0718

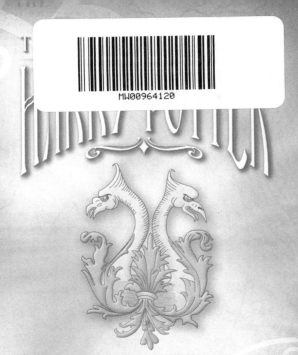

T

HARRY POTTER

G·U·I·D·E B·O·O·K
S E R I E S
Book 2 - The Chamber Of Secrets

Book 2 Synopsis

The second instalment in J.K. Rowling's Harry Potter series sees the twelve-year-old Harry returning to the Hogwarts academy for his second year of wizardry school. We join Harry at the Dursleys', where he is staying for the summer holidays. Spending time with his horrible muggle relatives is most unpleasant for Harry. His wand, broomstick and wizardry gear are locked away in the cupboard under the stairs. His owl Hedwig is not allowed outdoors, and he can't even do his summer homework assignments. The only saving grace for Harry is that Uncle Vernon and Aunt Petunia are afraid of his magical powers and live in constant fear of reprisals should they mistreat him. This leads to some hijinks by Harry, who can't resist pretending to cast spells on his cousin Dudley.

Unfortunately, Harry's game is up when the house-elf Dobby pays him a visit one night when the Dursleys are having important guests. Dobby begs Harry not to return to Hogwarts, where—so Dobby insists—his life will be in danger. When Harry is not deterred, Dobby resorts to desperate measures. He dashes downstairs and smashes the elegant dessert Aunt Petunia has prepared for her dinner party. The Dursleys are furious. Uncle Vernon loses the biggest deal of his career, and Harry—although he is innocent of

the charges—receives a notice from the Ministry of Magic, warning him against the use of magic while in the presence of muggles. The notice includes a reminder that performing spells out of school is not allowed.

Uncle Vernon is so angry at being deceived that he locks Harry up in his room for the rest of the holidays. Bars are installed on his window. A cat-flap in the door is used to deliver his scant meals. And he is only let out to use the bathroom.

Harry's troubles finally come to an end when his best friend Ron Weasley and Ron's twin brothers, Fred and George, come to his rescue in an old, turquoise flying car they have borrowed from their father. After using the car to pull away Harry's window bars and ordinary, muggle lock-picking to retrieve his gear from the cupboard under the stairs, they set off for The Burrow—the Weasleys' home. Harry spends the rest of his holidays in the enjoyable company of the Weasley family. He learns about garden gnomes and floo powder, and accidentally takes a trip to dangerous Knockturn Alley, whose shops are devoted to the dark arts.

Summer is soon over and the Weasley children and Harry prepare for their return to Hogwarts. Ron, Fred,

George, Percy, Ginny, and Harry load up the flying car with their books and school supplies and set out for King's Cross station to catch the Hogwarts Express. Unfortunately, Mrs. Weasley insists on driving muggle style—not flying—and they arrive very late. For some reason, Ron and Harry can't pass through the magical barrier to platform nine and three-quarters, and end up missing the train. There's nothing for it but to borrow Mr. Weasley's car and fly to school by following the Hogwarts Express.

Just before they reach Hogwarts, the flying car starts to sputter and cough. The engine dies, and Harry and Ron plummet downwards—right into the branches of the whomping willow. Both boys and car are soundly thrashed by the tree's lashing, flailing limbs, and poor Ron's wand is broken in the scuffle. When they finally break free, the long-suffering car ejects the boys and their luggage and takes off without a backward glance. Harry and Ron are in big trouble. Ron gets a stinging howler from his mother, and Professor McGonagall assigns detentions. Ron is set to help Mr. Filch hand-polish the silver in the trophy room. Harry is assigned to help the pompous Professor Lockhart answer his fan mail. It is when Harry is in Lockhart's second-floor office that he first hears the bone-chilling voice. And it's threatening to kill him.

Other than Harry's voices—which no one else can hear—the term begins rather uneventfully. Transfiguration class is spent trying to turn beetles into buttons. The earmuffed Herbology class transplants ugly, squirming mandrake seedlings. Destructive Cornish pixies are released in Professor Lockhart's class. And the first quidditch practice sees the Slytherins with a new seeker, Draco Malfoy.

Harry, Hermione and Ron accept an invitation to a deathday party in honour of Nearly Headless Nick's 500th on October 31. By the time the day comes around, they are beginning to regret their decision: it means they will miss the wonderful Halloween party in the great hall. But a promise is a promise, and the three friends dutifully head down to the dungeons for the deathday celebrations. Harry hears the murderous voice once again, and is convinced that its owner is going to kill someone. He follows the sound and comes upon a wall that bears an ominous inscription. Hanging from a torch bracket below the words is Mrs. Norris, Filch's cat, who has been petrified by dark magic.

Harry, Ron and Hermione resolve to find the perpetrator of the crime and figure out the meaning of the mysterious inscription. Their investigations lead them

to the story of the chamber of secrets, an ancient legend of a chamber that hides a horrible evil which will rid the school of all those who are not worthy to practice magic. According to the legend, only the true heir of Salazar Slytherin will be able to open the chamber. Unfortunately for Harry, many of his schoolmates believe that *he* is Slytherin's heir—and avoid him like the plague.

Harry and his friends are determined to find out the truth. Their first hunch is that Draco Malfoy is Slytherin's heir; Draco's disdain for muggle-born wizards is no secret. They decide to use a polyjuice potion to infiltrate Slytherin House and listen in on Draco's conversations. While they are laying their plans, Gryffindor defeats Slytherin in the first quidditch match of the season. A mad bludger ball breaks Harry's right arm, and to make matters worse, Professor Lockhart "helps" by removing Harry's broken bones instead of mending them.

During a painful night in hospital, where his bones regrow with the help of Madam Pomfrey's skele-gro, Harry gets another visit from Dobby the house-elf. A new patient is brought in during the night. It is pesky Colin Creevey, a first-year Gryffindor who is Harry's biggest

fan. Colin was found petrified in the dormitory, his ever-ready camera beside him.

Soon after Harry is released from hospital, a duelling club is established at Hogwarts. The young wizards face off with their wands and duel by sending spells at one another. Harry is paired with Draco Malfoy, who conjures a snake that attacks Justin Finch-Fletchley. To the amazement of the class, the snake obeys Harry's command to leave Justin alone. Harry realizes that he is a parselmouth—someone who can speak snake language—although this discovery only makes his fellow students more convinced that he is Slytherin's evil heir. It doesn't help that Justin is later found petrified next to a smoking, black Nearly Headless Nick.

By the Christmas holiday, the polyjuice potion is ready at last and Harry, Ron and Hermione lay their plans to spy on Malfoy. Things don't go exactly as planned, but the friends do learn that the chamber of secrets was last opened fifty years ago, that whoever opened it was expelled from Hogwarts, and that someone died. Eventually, the pieces of the puzzle begin to fall together—with help from a temperamental ghost named Moaning Myrtle, an

oversized and very hungry spider named Aragog, and a mysterious blank diary that once belonged to a student named Tom Riddle.

Harry continues to hear the murderous voice, and two more students—Hermione and Penelope Clearwater—are found petrified. Harry and Ron finally realize that it is a basilisk that is terrorizing the castle. When Ginny Weasley is kidnapped and taken to the chamber of secrets, they have no choice but to go after the monster. Harry uses his parselmouth ability to track the basilisk to the chamber, where he battles the heir of Slytherin in a last-ditch, no-holds-barred effort to rescue Ginny and save Hogwarts!

WHO'S WHO
AND WHAT'S WHAT

(All definitions are based on the characters and references
in J.K. Rowling's original Harry Potter books.)

Aparecium A spell that causes invisible ink to become readable.

Apothecary A bad-smelling but fascinating Diagon Alley shop which sells potion ingredients.

Apparate To instantly appear somewhere other than where you currently are. *See* **Apparition**.

Apparition Travelling by vanishing from one spot (disapparating) and instantly reappearing somewhere else (apparating).

Aragog A huge, old, black spider—now greying and blind—that was once a pet of Hagrid's. Aragog comes from a far-off land. He is the size of an elephant and has enormous clicking pincers. Hagrid got Aragog when he was just an egg. He raised him while he was a student at Hogwarts, feeding him table scraps and keeping him hidden in a cupboard in the castle. When Aragog was discovered and falsely accused of murder, Hagrid spirited him away to safety in the Forbidden Forest. His loyalty cost a great price. The Hogwarts authorities believed that Hagrid had released the monster in the chamber of secrets and expelled from school.

Nevertheless, Hagrid remained faithful to his friend and even found him a wife, Mosag. Aragog and his growing family still live in the forest, and Hagrid still comes to visit. *See* **Basilisk** *and* **Chamber of Secrets**.

Azkaban The wizard prison.

Basilisk Also known as the king of serpents. The deadliest of all monsters, the basilisk is an enormous snake born from a chicken's egg and hatched under a toad. It can live for hundreds of years and only fears a rooster's crowing, which is fatal to it. The basilisk has deadly fangs and can also kill its victims by petrifying them with a single glance. Spiders are mortally afraid of basilisks and will not even dare to speak the name. A basilisk dwells in Hogwarts' chamber of secrets. *See* **Aragog** *and* **Chamber of Secrets**.

Beater A quidditch position. A quidditch team has two beaters who protect their teammates from rocketing bludger balls. The beaters use a small club—like a baseball bat or a rounders bat—to knock the bludgers toward the opposing team. The Weasley twins, Fred and George, are the beaters for the Gryffindor team.

Bell, Katie One of the chasers on Gryffindor's quidditch team.

Bertie Bott's Every Flavour Beans Candy beans that come in ordinary flavours like chocolate, peppermint and marmalade, and unusual flavours like spinach, liver, tripe, sprouts, toast, coconut, baked bean, strawberry, curry, grass, coffee, sardine, pepper, earwax, and even vomit and bogey.

Bezoar A stone taken from the stomach of a goat. It protects against most poisons.

Binns, Professor A ghost who teaches Harry's boring History of Magic class at Hogwarts.

Blood-sucking Bugbear *See* **Bugbear, Blood-sucking**.

Bloody Baron A horrible, staring-eyed, gaunt-faced ghost whose robes are stained with silver blood. The Baron is Slytherin's resident ghost. He is the only one who can control the poltergeist Peeves.

Bludger One of the three types of balls used in quidditch. Bludger balls are jet black and slightly smaller than the red, soccer-ball-sized quaffle. Two bludger balls are

required for a quidditch game. The bludgers are self-propelled and rocket around trying to get past the beaters to knock players off their brooms. They have never killed anyone at Hogwarts, although casualties have included several broken jaws.

Boomslang Skin An ingredient in polyjuice potion. Hermione steals the required amount from Professor Snape's private stores.

Borgin and Burkes A Knockturn Alley shop that deals in illegal wizardry supplies and paraphernalia related to the dark arts.

Brown, Lavender One of Harry's Gryffindor classmates. Lavender is a good friend of Parvinder Patil.

Bugbear, Blood-sucking A creature that Hagrid suspects may be responsible for the mysterious death of his roosters.

Bulstrode, Millicent A Slytherin House member who started at Hogwarts the same year Harry did. Millicent is Hermione's partner in the duelling club. This gives Hermione the opportunity to get what she thinks is one of Millicent's hairs to use in polyjuice potion.

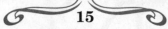

Burrow, The The Weasleys' house in Ottery St. Catchpole. One of its furnishings is a grandfather clock whose nine golden hands are engraved with the names of family members. Instead of pointing to numbers, the positions of the hands show where each Weasley might be—at home, at school, lost, and so on. The "mortal peril" position is at the top of the clock, where the number twelve would normally be. Another of The Burrow's clocks has only one hand, which points to the names of chores when it is time to do them. There's also a talking mirror and a ghoul who lives in the attic.

Cauldron Cake A type of wizard candy.

Chamber of Secrets A hidden chamber said to have been built by Salazar Slytherin, one of the founders of Hogwarts, who believed that only children from pure-blood wizarding families should be allowed to learn magic. According to legend, Slytherin sealed the chamber until such time as his "true heir" should arrive to open it and unleash its monster to purge Hogwarts of any and all deemed unworthy to study magic—that is, muggle-born and mixed-blood students. When the

chamber was first opened fifty years ago, a Hogwarts student was expelled and someone was killed. *See* **Basilisk**.

Chaser A quidditch position. A quidditch team has three chasers who score goals by getting the red quaffle ball through one of the three, fifty-foot-high golden hoops located at each end of the quidditch field. Each goal earns ten points. Angelina Johnson, Katie Bell and Alicia Spinnet are the chasers for the Gryffindor team.

Chocolate Frog A chocolate treat which comes with a trading card that shows famous witches and wizards, including Dumbledore, Circe, Cliodna (a druidess), Flamel (an alchemist), Alberic Grunnion, Hengist of Woodcroft, Merlin, Morgana, Paracelsus and others. As in all wizard pictures, the subjects can move around and sometimes even leave for a time.

Chudley Cannons Ron Weasley's favourite quidditch team, which is ninth in the league. The team's uniform is bright orange with two black C's and a speeding cannonball.

Cleansweep Seven An above-average flying-broom, but not quite as good as the Nimbus models.

Clearwater, Penelope A prefect from Ravenclaw House. Penelope is Percy Weasley's girlfriend. She is one of the victims of the basilisk who dwells in the chamber of secrets. Fortunately, she sees the creature through a mirror, so that her petrifaction is not permanent.

Coat of Arms, Hogwarts The school coat of arms bears the symbols of the four Hogwarts houses—an eagle (for Ravenclaw), a snake (for Slytherin), a lion (for Gryffindor), and a badger (for Hufflepuff)—surrounding a large letter H.

Comet Two Sixty An average flying-broom.

Committee on Experimental Charms A department in the Ministry of Magic.

Common Welsh Green A wild dragon native to Britain.

Cornish Pixie A shrill-voiced, destructive, electric-blue creature that stands approximately eight inches high. Pixies wreak havoc on their surroundings.

Crabbe, Vincent One of Draco Malfoy's muscular, thickset, mean-looking, brutish friends. Crabbe has a very thick

neck and his hair looks like it was cut around a bowl. He is somewhat taller than his friend Goyle. Crabbe and Goyle are Draco Malfoy's faithful sidekicks. They are in the same year as Harry and they all belong to Slytherin House.

Creevey, Colin A Hogwarts student who idolizes Harry and who is always following him around and trying to take his picture. Colin joins Gryffindor the year after Harry. His muggle father is a milkman. Colin is one of the victims of the basilisk who dwells in the chamber of secrets, but his camera saves him from permanent petrifaction.

Cupboard Under the Stairs This is Harry's room for the first ten years that he lives in the Dursley house on Privet Drive. It is small, dark, and infested with spiders. Harry finally gets his own room the summer he turns eleven, when the Dursleys realize that "somebody" magically knows about the cupboard under the stairs.

Daily Prophet The wizards' newspaper. The paper also has an evening edition called the *Evening Prophet*.

Dark Lord. *See* **Voldemort**.

De Mimsy-Porpington, Sir Nicholas The resident ghost of Gryffindor House; also known as Nearly Headless Nick because someone tried to behead him, but botched the job. Sir Nicholas was hit on the neck with a blunt axe forty-five times. His head is attached with just a bit of skin and he can pull it down to his shoulder by tugging on his left ear. Sir Nicholas has been dead since October 31, 1492. He wears a ruff, a doublet and hose, and a plumed hat, and he is always willing to help new students find their way around Hogwarts. One of his major disappointments is not being allowed to join the Headless Hunt.

Deathday Party Similar to a birthday party; celebrated by ghosts to mark the day of their death.

Deflating Draft A potion that counteracts the effects of swelling solution.

Delaney-Podmore, Sir Patrick The ghost who organizes the Headless Hunt.

Diagon Alley A cobbled London street where witches and wizards do their shopping. Specialty shops on Diagon

Alley include the Apothecary (for potion supplies), Madam Malkin's Robes for All Occasions, Eeylops Owl Emporium, Ollivanders (for wands), and Flourish and Blotts bookstore. The entrance to Diagon Alley is through a magical archway in the courtyard behind the Leaky Cauldron.

Dippet, Armando Headmaster at Hogwarts in Tom Riddle's time, when the chamber of secrets was first opened.

Disarming Spell A spell used to disarm a wizard by ejecting his wand from his possession. The magic word for the disarming spell is *expelliarmus*.

Dobby The Malfoy's house-elf, who tries to protect Harry by keeping him away from Hogwarts, where an evil plot is afoot and his life will be in danger. Dobby wears a grubby pillowcase and is constantly punishing himself for any hint of disloyalty to his master. Harry arranges to free Dobby from his life of servitude by tricking Malfoy into giving the house-elf a sock. *See* **House-elf**.

Dr. Filibuster's Fabulous Wet-Start, No-Heat Fireworks
A special sort of indoor fireworks that creates long-lasting red and blue stars which ricochet off walls and ceilings.

Drooble's Best Blowing Gum Magic bubble gum that makes blue bubbles which last for several days.

Dumbledore, Albus Headmaster of Hogwarts (Order of Merlin, First Class, Grand Sorcerer, Chief Warlock, Supreme Mugwump, International Confederation of Wizards). Dumbledore is a tall, thin, very old wizard whose silver hair and beard are both long enough to tuck into his belt. He has a very long, crooked nose that seems to have been broken at least twice. He has bright, sparkling, light-blue eyes and wears half-moon spectacles. A scar above his left knee shows a perfect map of the London subway system.

Dumbledore wears high-heeled, buckled boots, long robes, and a purple cloak which sweeps the ground. He carries a put-outer to control streetlights and wears a strange, twelve-handed gold watch that has little planets moving around the edge instead of numbers. He enjoys chamber music and tenpin bowling, and is fond of muggle sweets called sherbet lemons.

Dumbledore's office at Hogwarts is a beautiful circular room filled with curious instruments and portraits of old headmasters and headmistresses. Dumbledore's phoenix, the faithful Fawkes, has a special golden perch behind the door.

Dumbledore is particularly famous for his 1945 defeat of the dark wizard Grindelwald and for his discoveries about dragon's blood. He is also known for the work he and his partner, Nicolas Flamel, did in the field of alchemy. Many consider him to be the greatest wizard of modern times.

Dursley, Aunt Marge Vernon Dursley's muggle sister and Dudley's aunt. She stays in the Dursleys' guest room when she comes to visit. Aunt Marge hates Harry as much as her brother does.

Dursley, Dudley Harry's cousin. Dudley's doting parents, Petunia and Vernon, think he is the finest boy anywhere. Their pet names for him include "Duddy," "popkin," "sweetums," "Dinky Duddydums," and "Ickle Dudleykins." Dudley is a porky, pink-faced, fat-headed boy with small, watery blue eyes and smooth, blond

hair. He hates exercise unless it involves punching someone. He and his big, stupid friends attend Smeltings Secondary School.

Dudley and his parents are all muggles. They are ashamed of having a wizard in the family and they all hate Harry.

Dursley, Petunia Dudley's mother and wife of Vernon. Petunia Dursley is Harry's muggle aunt on his mother's side; Lily Potter was her sister. Petunia is a thin, bony, horse-faced blonde with an unusually long neck that comes in handy for spying on her neighbours.

Dursley, Vernon Dudley's muggle father; married to Harry's Aunt Petunia. Vernon Dursley is a big, beefy, purple-faced fellow with a very large black moustache and hardly any neck. Vernon works as a director at Grunnings, a local drill-manufacturing firm. His office is on the ninth floor and he always works with his back to the window.

Elf *See* **House-elf**.

Eeylops Owl Emporium The place to shop for an owl. It is located in Diagon Alley and stocks tawny, screech, barn, brown and snowy owls.

Engorgement Charm Used to blow things up to maximum size. Hagrid grows boulder-sized pumpkins with the aid of an engorgement charm.

Errol The Weasley family's elderly, feeble, grey owl.

Evening Prophet The evening edition of the wizards' newspaper, *Daily Prophet*.

Expelliarmus The magic word for the disarming spell, which is used to eject a wand from another wizard's possession.

Exploding Snap A card game.

Fang Hagrid's huge black boarhound. Fang is far less ferocious than he looks.

Fat Friar One of Hogwarts' resident ghosts. The friar is a former student of Hufflepuff House.

Fat Lady A very fat woman in a pink silk dress whose portrait guards the entrance to Gryffindor House. *See* **Gryffindor**.

Fawkes Dumbledore's pet phoenix. Fawkes brings Harry the sorting hat and Godric Gryffindor's sword to help him in his battle with Tom Riddle.

Filch, Argus Hogwarts' bulgy-eyed, ill-tempered caretaker. Filch is reputed to know Hogwarts' secret passageways better than anyone. He and his cat, Mrs. Norris, patrol the hallways and try to catch students who are breaking the rules. Filch has a list of over four hundred forbidden objects posted outside his office door. He is not a proper wizard (he's a squib), but he is trying to learn magic by correspondence.

Filibuster fireworks *See* **Dr. Filibuster's Fabulous Wet-Start, No-Heat Fireworks**.

Finch-Fletchley, Justin A Hogwarts student in the same year as Harry. Justin belongs to Hufflepuff House, although his muggle-born parents thought he would go to Eton. Harry saves Justin from an attack by a snake conjured by Draco Malfoy. Justin later becomes one of the victims of the basilisk who dwells in the chamber of secrets. Nearly Headless Nick shields him from the creature's direct gaze and saves him from permanent petrifaction.

Finite Incantarum A spell which stops the effect of a previous enchantment.

Finnigan, Seamus One of Harry's Gryffindor classmates. Seamus' mother is a witch, but she didn't tell her muggle husband (Seamus' dad) until after they were married. Seamus has sandy hair.

Fletcher, Mundungus An old wizard who tries to hex Arthur Weasley when his back is turned.

Flint, Marcus Captain of Slytherin's quidditch team. Flint plays the position of chaser.

Flitwick, Professor Hogwarts' Charms teacher. Professor Flitwick is so tiny that he has to stand on a pile of books to see over his desk.

Floo Powder A sparkling powder that facilitates travelling from one wizard fire to another. When floo powder is thrown into a fire, the flames turn emerald-green. The traveller simply speaks the name of his intended destination, steps into the flames, and is instantly transported. When travelling by floo powder, it's important to speak clearly and to get out at the right

grate. It's also a good idea to keep your elbows in and your eyes and mouth shut. (Breathing in hot ash is not very pleasant.)

Flourish and Blotts The wizard bookstore located in Diagon Alley. This is where Hogwarts students buy their school texts. The bookstore shelves are stacked from floor to ceiling with volumes ranging from postage-stamp- to paving-stone-sized.

Flying Car A rusty old turquoise-coloured Ford Anglia that Mr. Weasley buys on the pretext of wanting to take it apart to see how it works. To the chagrin of his wife, he enchants the car so that it can fly, taking advantage of a loophole in the wizard law that prohibits meddling in muggle affairs. While it is illegal to fly a car, it is not illegal merely to have a car that can fly. Mr. Weasley's flying car has an enchanted interior that can easily accommodate eight people and all their luggage and pets. It is equipped with an invisibility booster that is activated by pressing a silver button. After an encounter with the whomping willow, the flying car ends its days running wild in the Forbidden Forest.

Forbidden Forest A forest on the grounds of Hogwarts. It is off limits to students because it is full of dangerous beasts.

Freezing Charm A charm used to immobolize. Hermione uses a freezing charm to control the Cornish pixies unleashed in Professor Lockhart's Defence Against the Dark Arts class.

Fudge, Cornelius Head of the Ministry of Magic. Fudge is a portly little man who likes to wear pinstriped suits, coats or cloaks; a scarlet tie; a lime-green bowler hat; and pointed purple boots. He relies heavily on Albus Dumbledore's advice and sends him owls every morning.

Galleon A gold coin used as wizard money. There are seventeen silver sickles or four hundred and ninety-three bronze knuts to a gold galleon.

Gambol and Japes Wizarding Joke Shop One of the specialty shops located in Diagon Alley.

Gnome A small, leathery, not-too-bright creature with horny little feet, sharp teeth and a bumpy bald head. Gnomes live in holes in people's gardens, which can be

de-gnomed if the creatures are caught by the ankles, swung around until they are dizzy, and tossed as far away as possible. This is usually a temporary solution, until the gnomes find their way back.

Goblin A small, swarthy creature with a clever face, pointed beard, and very long fingers and feet. Goblins are a head shorter than a small eleven-year-old. They run Gringotts, the wizards' bank, and are not to be messed with. Goblins speak the language Gobbledegook.

Godric's Hollow Where Harry lived with his parents, Lily and James Potter, until they were killed by Voldemort.

Golden Snitch The most important of the three types of balls used in quidditch. The tiny, bright-gold snitch has fluttering silver wings. It is only the size of a walnut and therefore very hard to see and catch. When the seeker succeeds in catching the snitch, the team earns one hundred and fifty points and the match ends.

Goyle, Gregory One of Draco Malfoy's thickset, mean-looking, brutish friends. Malfoy and his sidekicks, Crabbe and Goyle, are in the same year as Harry. They all belong to Slytherin House.

Granger, Hermione A Gryffindor who is best friends with Harry Potter and Ron Weasley. Hermione is an excellent student even though her parents (both dentists) are muggles. Hermione has bushy brown hair, a bossy voice, and rather large front teeth. Her name is pronounced Her-MY-oh-nee.

Hermione has an unfortunate accident when she first experiments with polyjuice potion: she ends up turning into a cat rather than into Millicent Bulstrode, as planned. She also falls victim to the basilisk who dwells in the chamber of secrets. Fortunately, she sees the creature through a mirror, so that her petrifaction is not permanent.

Great Hall A huge, grand room where Hogwarts school ceremonies and assemblies are held. Students sit at four long tables lit by thousands of candles that float in mid-air. Teachers sit at another long table at the top of the hall. Sumptuous feasts magically appear on golden plates. The ceiling is bewitched to look like the sky, and at night, its velvety blackness is dotted with stars.

Gringotts The wizards' goblin-run bank, which is heavily protected by spells and enchantments. Next to

Hogwarts, Gringotts is the safest place in the world. It is rumoured that dragons guard its high-security vaults, which are located hundreds of miles beneath the London subway system. Aboveground, Gringotts is a snowy-white building which towers above the shops in Diagon Alley. A goblin garbed in scarlet and gold stands guard at its burnished bronze doors. Inside, engraved silver doors open onto a vast, marble hall where a hundred goblins sit on high stools behind a very long counter—weighing coins, examining jewels, or scribbling away in ledgers. Goblin guides escort customers along narrow, twisting, underground passages to their vaults, which are reached by small railway carts that seem to know their own way.

Grunnings The drill-manufacturing company where Vernon Dursley is a director. Dursley's office is on the ninth floor.

Gryffindor, Godric One of the four founders of Hogwarts. Godric's gleaming, silver, ruby-hilted sword helps Harry overcome Tom Riddle. *See* **Fawkes** *and* **Hogwarts School of Witchcraft and Wizardry**.

Gryffindor One of the four Hogwarts houses; established by Godric Gryffindor, who valued bravery above all other virtues. Albus Dumbledore was once a member of this house. Gryffindor's colours are scarlet and gold and its emblem is a gold lion on a scarlet ground. Professor McGonagall is the head of the house. Sir Nicholas de Mimsy-Porpington is the resident ghost. The entrance to Gryffindor House is covered by a portrait of the Fat Lady, who needs to hear the secret password before her portrait swings open to uncover a round hole in the wall. The hole opens onto Gryffindor's round, common room. Boys' and girls' dormitories are located in a tower on top of a spiral staircase. Harry's room holds five four-poster beds hung with curtains of deep-red velvet. *See* **Fat Lady**.

Hagrid, Rubeus Keeper of Keys and Grounds at Hogwarts. Hagrid is a soft-hearted giant of a man—twice as tall and five times as wide as a normal person. His hands are the size of dustbin lids and his feet, the size of baby dolphins. He is a muscular, wild-looking fellow with beetle-black eyes, shaggy black hair, and a beard that hides most of his face. He is a notoriously bad cook, and his trademark is an oversize black moleskin coat.

Hagrid is especially fond of large, rather dangerous animals. He has a pet boarhound named Fang and a three-headed dog he calls Fluffy. He once tried to raise a giant spider named Aragog and a Norwegian ridgeback dragon named Norbert.

Hagrid lives in a cottage at the edge of the Forbidden Forest. He is a former Hogwarts student who was expelled in his third year for a crime he did not commit. His wand was broken as a result, and he is not supposed to do any magic. Nevertheless, he has the trust of Dumbledore, even though his pink umbrella sometimes causes strange phenomena that he asks his friends not to mention.

Hagrid is especially fond of Harry. When Harry's parents are killed, it is Hagrid who delivers the one-year-old orphan to the Dursleys' on a flying motorcycle borrowed from Sirius Black. Hagrid is also the one who finally delivers Harry's invitation to attend Hogwarts. He buys Harry his first real birthday present (his snowy owl Hedwig) and presents him with an album of photographs of his parents.

Hand of Glory A withered hand used by robbers. When a candle is inserted, the hand gives light only to its holder. It is available for sale at Borgin and Burkes in Knockturn Alley.

He-Who-Must-Not-Be-Named *See* **Voldemort**.

Headless Hunt A ghostly entertainment organized by Sir Patrick Delaney-Podmore. The hunt includes activities such as horseback head-juggling and head polo. Only ghosts whose heads are completely detached from their bodies may participate.

Hedwig Harry's snowy owl. She was a gift from Hagrid on Harry's eleventh birthday. Harry found her name in *A History of Magic*. He uses her to send messages.

Hermes Percy Weasley's owl. *See* **Weasley, Ron**.

Hogwarts Express The scarlet steam engine that transports students to and from Hogwarts each term. The train leaves from platform nine and three-quarters at London's King's Cross station at precisely 11 o'clock every September 1.

Hogwarts School of Witchcraft and Wizardry One of the finest schools of wizardry in the world, Hogwarts is situated atop a high mountain on the shore of a great black lake inhabited by a giant squid. The forest on the grounds is full of dangerous beasts and is forbidden territory to all pupils.

Hogwarts was founded over a thousand years ago by Godric Gryffindor, Helga Hufflepuff, Rowena Ravenclaw and Salazar Slytherin—the four greatest wizards and witches of their age. Together, they built a huge, magical, turreted castle with enormous meeting rooms, halls, mazes, secret rooms, temperamental doors (some of which need to be tickled before they open), and a hundred and forty-two staircases—including some with vanishing steps. Each of the founders established a house and chose students who exemplified the virtues they valued most. Gryffindor prized bravery, nerve and chivalry; Hufflepuff, loyalty, integrity and hard work; Ravenclaw, wit and learning; and Slytherin, cunning and ambition. While the founders were alive, they selected worthy students for each of their houses. Gryffindor enchanted his own hat—which became the sorting hat—so that it could make the selections once

he and his fellow founders were dead and gone. By Harry Potter's time, the sorting hat chooses the house to which new students will belong.

Each Hogwarts house has its own symbol and its own colours. Students' triumphs earn points for their respective houses, while students who misbehave and break rules lose house points. The competition between houses is quite intense because, at the end of the year, the house with the most points is awarded the coveted house cup.

The Hogwarts school song is sung to each student's favourite tune, so everyone finishes at a different time. Official school correspondence is written in emerald-green ink and sealed with purple wax bearing the school's coat of arms. The school term begins on September 1. It takes seven years to complete the Hogwarts course of studies.

Hogwarts castle is protected by a variety of enchantments, and it is considered one of the safest places on earth. Its location is invisible to muggles, who see only old ruins and signs warning people to keep out.

Hooch, Madam Hogwarts' teacher of broom-flying. Madam has short, grey hair and yellow, hawk-like eyes.

Hopkirk, Mafalda An officer in the Improper Use of Magic Office at the Ministry of Magic. It is she who reprimands the innocent Harry for using a hover charm at the Dursley House.

Hornby, Olive A student at Hogwarts during Tom Riddle's time. Olive liked to tease Moaning Myrtle about her glasses.

House-elf A rather ugly, doll-sized creature with a long, thin nose; bat-like ears; enormous, tennis-ball-sized eyes; and a high-pitched voice. House-elves are usually owned by wealthy old wizarding families. They are unswervingly loyal to their masters, and although they have powerful magic, they must use it only with their masters' permission. House-elves can only be freed if their masters present them with an article of clothing, which is why they are always seen in rags. Unless they are set free, they are bound to serve their master's house and family until they die.

Hover Charm The spell Harry is accused of performing at the Dursley house on his twelfth birthday.

Howler A scalding letter that is delivered by owl post. It begins to scream and yell as soon as it is opened. A howler that is not opened immediately will explode.

Hufflepuff, Helga One of the four founders of Hogwarts. *See* **Hogwarts School of Witchcraft and Wizardry**.

Hufflepuff One of the four Hogwarts houses; established by Helga Hufflepuff, who valued loyalty and hard work above all other virtues. Hufflepuff's colours are black and yellow and its emblem is a black badger on a yellow ground.

Improper Use of Magic Office A department in the Ministry of Magic. One of its duties is to ensure that underage wizards do not perform spells outside of school.

Invisibility Cloak A magical cloak that makes its wearer invisible.

Johnson, Angelina One of the chasers on Gryffindor's quidditch team.

Jordan, Lee A Gryffindor boy who sometimes serves as the commentator for quidditch games. Lee is a good friend of the Weasley twins.

Keeper A quidditch position. The keeper tries to stop the other team's chasers from getting the quaffle ball through the hoops in a quidditch match.

Knockturn Alley A dingy London alley whose shops are devoted to the dark arts.

Knut A small bronze coin used as wizard money. There are twenty-nine bronze knuts to a silver sickle.

Kwikspell A correspondence course in beginners' magic.

Leaky Cauldron A tiny, inconspicuous, grubby-looking London pub which is invisible to muggles. The pub serves as the entrance to Diagon Alley, where many wizard shops are found. Access is through a magical archway which appears when a particular brick in the wall of the rear courtyard is tapped three times. The special brick is three up and two across from the dustbin. When the brick is tapped, it quivers and

wriggles until a hole appears and grows into a large archway that opens onto Diagon Alley. Once travellers step through, the hole disappears.

Liquorice Wand A type of wizard candy.

Little Whinging The Surrey community where the Dursleys live.

Lockhart, Gilderoy Hogwarts' Defence Against the Dark Arts teacher in Harry's second year at the school. Lockhart is a handsome but conceited man with wavy blond hair and blue eyes. Although an incompetent wizard, he is the author of a number of popular books, including *Gilderoy Lockhart's Guide to Household Pests*. He has also written an autobiography called *Magical Me* and a number of texts—*Break with a Banshee*, *Gadding with Ghouls*, *Holidays with Hags*, *Travels with Trolls*, *Voyages with Vampires*, *Wanderings with Werewolves*, and *Year with the Yeti*—that are prescribed for second-year Hogwarts students. Lockhart has won the *Witch Weekly's* Most-Charming-Smile Award five times in a row and his achievements include the Order of Merlin, Third Class and honorary membership in the Dark Force Defence

League. He favours bright robes and hats in turquoise, aquamarine and other shades of blue. He dresses in shocking pink in honour of Valentine's Day, and his favourite colour is lilac.

Longbottom, Neville One of Harry's Gryffindor classmates. Round-faced, accident-prone, forgetful Neville lives with his grandmother, who is delighted when he finally shows some aptitude for wizardry at the age of eight. It happens when his Great Uncle Algie drops him out of an upstairs window by mistake. To everyone's delight, Neville bounces! Uncle Algie is so pleased that he buys him a toad, Trevor. Neville's grandmother gives him a remembrall to help him remember things, but Neville is still forgetful and not very good at Charms or Potions. Herbology is his best subject.

Lumos The magic word that causes the end of a wizard's wand to light up.

Macmillan, Ernie One of Harry's schoolmates. Ernie is a pure-blood wizard who belongs to Hufflepuff House. He is convinced that Harry is the heir of Slytherin, but later apologizes.

Madam Malkin's Robes for All Occasions The robe-maker's shop in Diagon Alley. The proprietor is a squat, smiling witch robed in mauve.

Malfoy, Draco A conceited, sneaky bully whom Harry hates even more than his porky cousin Dudley. Malfoy has a pale, pointed face. He belongs to Slytherin House and is rarely seen without his brutish sidekicks, Crabbe and Goyle. In his second year at Hogwarts, Draco is given the position of seeker on the Slytherin Quidditch team. His appointment is not due to talent, but to the fact that his father has bought the whole team new Nimbus Two Thousand and One flying-brooms.

Malfoy, Lucius Draco's father. Lucius is a former supporter of Voldemort. He makes a show of abandoning the dark arts after his master is overthrown, but his true allegiance is suspect. When the new Muggle Protection Act is passed, Lucius unloads some of the illegal items in his possession at Borgin and Burkes. He plants Tom Riddles diary on Ginny Weasley during a scuffle with Ginny's father at Flourish and Botts.

Mandragora *See* **Mandrake**.

Mandrake Also known as mandragora; a dangerous plant that nevertheless has powerful restorative properties and is used in most antidotes. The root of a mandrake seedling is an ugly, kicking, pale-green, mottled-skinned baby with purplish-green leaves growing out of its head. Mature mandrake roots look like grown-up people, and their cry is fatal to anyone who hears it. The cries of seedlings won't kill, but they will render their hearers unconscious for several hours. Protective earmuffs must be worn when working with mandrakes. *See* **Mandrake Restorative Draught**.

Mandrake Restorative Draught A potion made from the mandrake plant. It can restore transfigured or cursed individuals back to their original state.

Mason, Mr. and Mrs. The Dursleys' dinner guests on the night Dobby comes to visit.

McGonagall, Minerva Professor, deputy headmistress, and head of Gryffindor House. McGonagall is a tall, severe-looking woman who favours emerald-green robes and cloaks. She wears square eyeglasses and pulls her black hair back into a tight bun. Strict and

clever, McGonagall is definitely not a teacher to cross. She teaches transfiguration and can change shape at will. She has often disguised herself as a cat.

Memory Charm A charm that erases memories. It is frequently used on muggles who have witnessed wizard phenomena they should not have seen. Memory modification can be a somewhat disorienting experience. The magic word used for the memory charm is *obliviate*.

Ministry of Magic A multi-department agency headed by Cornelius Fudge. One of the ministry's roles is keeping muggles unaware that there are witches and wizards everywhere. The ministry also regulates underage wizards, experimental charms, magical creatures, international relations, magical games and sport, and the improper use of magic.

Moaning Myrtle A Hogwarts ghost who is prone to throwing tantrums. Myrtle haunts a toilet in the girl's first-floor bathroom, where her fits often end up flooding the place. Fifty years ago, Myrtle met her death in the bathroom she now haunts. She had hidden in a stall to cry when Olive Hornby teased her about

her glasses. She heard a boy speaking in a strange tongue, and the next thing she knew, she had died— a victim of the dreaded basilisk.

Mosag Wife of the giant spider Aragog.

Moste Potente Potions The library book in which Hermione finds the recipe for polyjuice potion.

Mudblood An insulting name for a witch or wizard who has non-magic (muggle) parents.

Muggle A non-magic person.

Nearly Headless Nick *See* **De Mimsy-Porpington, Sir Nicholas**.

Nimbus Two Thousand One of the best and fastest flying-brooms made.

Nimbus Two Thousand and One A new and improved version of the Nimbus Two Thousand.

Norris, Mrs. Mr. Filch's scrawny, bulgy-eyed, dust-coloured cat. She patrols the halls of Hogwarts and reports to Filch if she sees anyone misbehaving. Hogwarts students are not too fond of Mrs. Norris.

Number Four, Privet Drive The Dursleys' house in Little Whinging, Surrey (in southeast England).

Obliviate The magic word for the memory charm.

Ollivanders A wand shop located in Diagon Alley. The Ollivanders have been makers of fine wands since 382 BC. "The wand chooses the wizard," according to Mr. Ollivander, and no two Ollivander wands are quite the same. Each has a core made from a powerful magical substance. The core of Voldemort's thirteen-and-a-half-inch yew wand is a phoenix feather. Harry's eleven-inch holly wand contains a feather from the same phoenix. These two feathers are the only ones this particular phoenix has ever given.

Ottery St. Catchpole The village where the Weasleys live.

O.W.L. Ordinary Wizarding Level examinations taken by Hogwarts students when they are fifteen (in their fifth year).

Owl Post The wizards' "airmail" messenger service.

Parselmouth Someone who has the ability to talk to snakes. Salazar Slytherin was a famous parselmouth, which is

why the symbol of Slytherin House is a snake. Harry Potter is also a parselmouth.

Parseltongue The language used by snakes.

Patil, Parvati One of Harry's Gryffindor classmates. Parvati's twin sister, Padma, is also a Hogwarts student. Parvati and Lavender Brown are good friends.

Peeves A nasty little poltergeist with dark, wicked eyes and a wide mouth. Peeves wears an orange bow tie and a hat covered in bells. He delights in mischief of all sorts, from stuffing keyholes with chewing gum to throwing water balloons at unsuspecting students. Peeves makes life particularly difficult for first-years. He gives them wrong directions, drops and throws things at them, pulls rugs out from under their feet, and sneaks up behind and grabs their noses. Only the Bloody Baron can control him.

Perkins An old warlock who is Arthur Weasley's colleague in the Misuse of Muggle Artifacts Office at the Ministry of Magic.

Pepper-up Potion Madam Pomfrey's cold remedy and general tonic. It works instantly, but the drinker's ears smoke for several hours after.

Peskipiksi Pesternomi The incantation Lockhart uses when he tries to subdue the Cornish pixies released in his classroom. It has no effect.

Phoenix A remarkable, swan-sized bird that bursts into flame when it is time for it to die, and is reborn from its own ashes. Phoenixes have glorious red and gold plumage and golden talons. Their tears have the power to heal, and they can carry very heavy loads. They make extremely faithful pets.

Pince, Madam Hogwarts' thin, irritable librarian, who looks a bit like a vulture.

Pixie, Cornish *See* **Cornish Pixie**.

Platform Nine and Three-quarters Located at King's Cross station in London. The Hogwarts Express leaves from this platform at 11 o'clock sharp every September 1. The platform is reached by walking straight through the ticket barrier between muggle platforms nine and ten.

Polyjuice Potion A complicated potion that, for a short time, transforms the person who drinks it into someone else. Polyjuice takes a month to prepare. It requires lacewing flies that have been stewed for twenty-one days, leeches, fluxweed picked at the full moon, knotgrass, powdered bicorn horn, shredded boomslang skin, and a bit of whoever you want to transform into. The recipe can be found in the book *Most Potente Potions*.

Pomfrey, Poppy Madam Pomfrey is the Hogwarts school physician.

Potter, Harry Born on July 31, Harry is the orphaned son of James and Lily Potter, who are killed by the evil Voldemort when Harry is just a year old. When his parents are killed, Albus Dumbledore asks Hagrid to bring Harry to live with his only relatives, Vernon and Petunia Dursley and their young son Dudley. Petunia is a sister to Harry's mother, Lily. The Dursleys are muggles (non-magic folk) who despise wizards and magic. They fear Harry and treat him badly.

Harry is a small, skinny boy with a thin face and rather knobby knees. He has his father's unruly, jet-black hair and his mother's green eyes. He wears round glasses,

and his most distinguishing feature is a thin, lightning-bolt-shaped scar on his forehead. This is the legacy of Voldemort's unsuccessful attempt to kill him when he was a baby. Harry is the only wizard ever to have survived an attack by Voldemort. *See also:* **Hagrid, Rubeus**; **Ollivanders**; *and* **Voldemort**.

Potter, James and Lily Harry's parents, both of whom were powerful wizards. Lily and James were killed by the evil Voldemort on Halloween night when Harry was one year old, but Lily managed to protect her son. Red-haired, green-eyed Lily Potter was Petunia Dursley's sister and muggle-born. James Potter was a tall, thin man with untidy black hair and glasses. The Potters lived at Godric's Hollow.

Potter, Lily *See* **Potter, James and Lily**.

Privet Drive *See* **Number 4, Privet Drive**.

Pumpkin Pasty A pumpkin-flavoured turnover.

Quaffle One of the three types of balls used in quidditch. The bright-red quaffle is about the size of a soccer ball. Ten points are earned each time a chaser manages to get the quaffle through one of the opposing team's hoops.

Quidditch This is the wizards' national sport, which is played on flying broomsticks. There are seven hundred ways to commit a quidditch foul. There are seven players on a quidditch team: three chasers, two beaters, a keeper, and a seeker. A quidditch field (also called a pitch) has three fifty-foot-high golden hoops at each end The chasers try to get the red, soccer-ball-sized quaffle through the hoops to score ten points. The keeper tries to prevent the opposing team from scoring. The keeper is assisted by two black bludger balls which rocket around trying to knock players off their brooms. The beaters knock the bludgers away with small clubs that look like baseball or rounders bats. The seeker chases the tiny, silver-winged golden snitch, which is very hard to see and catch. (The record is three months.) Capturing the snitch earns one hundred and fifty points and ends the game. The game is not over until the snitch has been caught.

Ravenclaw, Rowena One of the four founders of Hogwarts. *See* **Hogwarts School of Witchcraft and Wizardry**.

Ravenclaw One of the four Hogwarts houses; established by Rowena Ravenclaw, who valued wit and learning

above all other virtues. Ravenclaw's colours are blue and bronze and its emblem is a bronze eagle on a blue ground.

Revealer A bright-red, magic eraser that, when used on invisible ink, causes it to appear.

Rictusempra The magic word used for the tickling charm, which paralyzes its victim with laughter.

Riddle, Tom Marvolo A student at Hogwarts fifty years before Harry's time. Tom's mother was a witch who named him for his muggle father (Tom Sr.) and grandfather. She died just after Tom was born, and he was raised in an orphanage. During his time at Hogwarts, Tom won an award for special service to the school. The true heir of Slytherin, he also opened the chamber of secrets and released the fearsome basilisk that killed Moaning Myrtle.

When Harry Potter is in his second year at Hogwarts, Tom arranges for him to discover his diary as a way of luring him to the chamber of secrets and certain death. The pages of the diary seem blank, but when Harry unlocks their secret, he is able to correspond with Tom.

Tom convinces Harry that it was Hagrid who opened the chamber fifty years ago. In reality, it was Tom, who has now enchanted young Ginny Weasley and controls her movements. It is Ginny who has reopened the chamber of secrets and released the dreaded basilisk. When Ginny is kidnapped, Harry meets Tom, only to discover that he is really Lord Voldemort. His name, Tom Marvolo Riddle, is an anagram for the words "I am Lord Voldemort." *See* **Malfoy, Lucius**; **Vauxhall Road**; **Voldemort** *and* **Weasley, Ginny**.

Riddle, Tom Sr. Voldemort's muggle father.

Rowling, J.K. Joanne Kathleen (Jo) Rowling, author of the Harry Potter series. Rowling was born in Chipping Sodbury in the UK in 1965. She studied French at the University of Exeter in Devon. She later taught French in Edinburgh, where she currently lives with her daughter.

Scabbers Ron Weasley's fat, gray rat, which used to belong to his brother Percy. Ron got Scabbers when Percy received an owl as a reward for becoming a prefect.

Seeker A quidditch position. The seeker's job is to capture the tiny, silver-winged, golden snitch. Capturing the snitch earns one hundred and fifty points and ends the game.

Serpensortia The magic word used to conjure a snake.

Shooting Star A second-rate flying-broom which even has trouble keeping up with butterflies.

Sickle A silver coin used as wizard money. There are seventeen silver sickles to a gold galleon, and twenty-nine bronze knuts to a silver sickle.

Skele-gro A steaming, throat-burning medicine that regrows bones. (Bone regrowing is a painful process.)

Slytherin, Salazar One of the four founders of Hogwarts and a noted parselmouth. Slytherin believed that magical learning should be restricted to all-magic families and that muggle-born students should be excluded. His views eventually led to a falling out with the other founders, and he left Hogwarts. *See* **Hogwarts School of Witchcraft and Wizardry**.

Slytherin One of the four Hogwarts houses; established by Salazar Slytherin, who valued cunning and ambition

above all other virtues. Slytherin's colours are green and silver and its emblem is a silver snake on a green ground.

Smallest Bedroom Harry's room at the Dursleys'; formerly Dudley's second bedroom, where he kept all the toys that didn't fit into his first bedroom. *See* **Cupboard Under the Stairs**.

Snape, Severus Professor and head of Slytherin House. Snape is the Potions instructor, but he really wants to be teaching Defence Against the Dark Arts. His classes are held in a cold, creepy dungeon stocked with pickled animals floating in glass jars. Snape has greasy black hair, a hooked nose, sallow skin and cold, empty black eyes. Harry is convinced that Snape hates him. He eventually learns why. Snape attended Hogwarts with Harry Potter's father James, whom he always resented. However, James Potter saved Snape's life when a practical joke went wrong, and Snape owes him (and therefore his son) a grudging debt.

Snitch *See* **Golden Snitch**.

Sorting Hat A frayed, patched and very dirty pointed wizard's hat that belonged to Godric Gryffindor, one of

the founders of Hogwarts. New students take part in a sorting ceremony during which the sorting hat is placed on their heads. The hat decides which Hogwarts house each student will belong to. *See* **Fawkes** *and* **Hogwarts School of Witchcraft and Wizardry**.

Spellotape What wizards use for mending rips and tears in books and the like. Ron Weasley repairs his broken wand with spellotape.

Spinnet, Alicia One of the chasers on Gryffindor's quidditch team.

Sprout, Professor A squat little witch with flyaway hair under a patched hat. She teaches Herbology, and usually has earth on her clothes and fingernails.

Squib Someone who has no magical powers in spite of having been born into a wizarding family. Squibs are quite unusual.

Swelling Solution A potion that causes swelling. Learning to make it is part of the second-year Hogwarts curriculum.

Tarantallegra A magic word which can make someone dance a quickstep.

Tickling Charm A charm which paralyzes its victim with laughter. The magic word for the tickling charm is *rictusempra*.

The Burrow *See* **Burrow, The**.

Thomas, Dean One of Harry's Gryffindor classmates.

Transfiguration Complex, dangerous magic used to turn one thing into something else. Professor McGonagall teaches the Transfiguration class at Hogwarts.

Vauxhall Road The location of the London variety store where Tom Riddle's diary was purchased.

Voldemort A powerful wizard who goes bad and terrorizes the wizard world, killing all who oppose him and recruiting followers to the dark side. Most wizards fear him so much that they never refer to him by name, but rather, as You-Know-Who or He-Who-Must-Not-Be-Named or the dark lord. Albus Dumbledore is the only wizard Voldemort fears and one of the few who dare to speak his name.

Voldemort kills Harry's parents, James and Lily Potter, and tries to kill the one-year-old Harry as well. His

murderous green blast leaves Harry with his lightning-shaped scar, but bounces back on Voldemort, turning him into mere shadow and vapour.

For many years after the attack, Voldemort can only take on human form when he shares another body. He needs unicorn's blood and the philosopher's stone to regain his former power, but Harry Potter keeps him from getting the needed ingredients. Voldemort attempts another comeback by using his old diary to lure Harry to the chamber of secrets. With the help of the phoenix Fawkes, Harry overcomes the dark lord yet again and destroys the diary with the venomous fang of a basilisk. *See* **Fawkes**; **Ollivanders**; **Potter, James and Lily**; *and* **Riddle, Tom Marvolo**.

Warbeck, Celestina A popular singing sorceress who is often featured on the radio show "Witching Hour."

Weasley, Arthur and Molly Ron's parents. Ron's mother, Molly, is a short, plump, kindly woman who conjures wonderful meals and often carries a large clothes brush in her bag. Mrs. Weasley sends Harry and her children homemade sweets and hand-knitted sweaters (jumpers) each Christmas. Ron's sweater is always maroon, which

he hates. Arthur Weasley is a thin, balding man who wears glasses. All seven of his children have inherited his red hair. Arthur heads the Misuse of Muggle Artifacts Office at the Ministry of Magic and is fascinated by muggles and muggle affairs. The Weasleys don't have much money. They live outside a village called Ottery St. Catchpole in a house called The Burrow. Their ancient owl, Errol, delivers their messages.

Weasley, Bill The oldest of Ron's red-headed brothers. Bill used to be the Gryffindor head boy. He is now in Egypt, working as a curse-breaker for Gringotts (the wizards' bank). Bill is tall and wears his long hair tied back in a ponytail. He is a fashionable dresser who sports a fang earring and dragonhide boots.

Weasley, Charlie The second-oldest of Ron's red-headed brothers and an alumnus of Hogwarts. Charlie was captain of Gryffindor's quidditch team. Stockily built like his twin brothers, good-natured Charlie has a very freckled and weather-beaten broad face. He is now studying dragons in Romania.

Weasley, Fred and George Ron's older brothers, who are identical, red-headed twins. Although the twins are

always getting into trouble and constantly scheming up new tricks, they both get really good grades. Fred and George are beaters on Gryffindor's quidditch team. They are shorter and stockier than their brothers Percy and Ron.

Weasley, George *See* **Weasley, Fred and George**.

Weasley, Ginny The youngest member of the Weasley family and the only girl. Like all of her siblings, Ginny has red hair. Ginny starts at Hogwarts when her brother Ron is in his second year, and is selected for Gryffindor House. She falls under the control of Tom Riddle (Voldemort), who causes her to do all sorts of terrible things—from killing Hagrid's roosters to opening the chamber of secrets and unleashing the dreaded basilisk. Riddle manipulates Ginny through his magical diary, which Lucius Malfoy manages to plant inside one of her schoolbooks. Ginny has had a crush on Harry from the time she first saw him, and her admiration for him only grows when he rescues her from the clutches of the dark lord. *See* **Basilisk**; **Malfoy, Lucius**; **Riddle, Tom Marvolo**; *and* **Voldemort**.

Weasley, Molly *See* **Weasley, Arthur and Molly**.

Weasley, Percy One of Ron's red-headed older brothers. Tall, lanky Percy is a prefect at Hogwarts, and he wears his shiny, silver prefect's badge everywhere he goes. He is older than the twins and is always fussing about school rules and regulations. Like all the other Weasleys, Percy belongs to Gryffindor House.

Weasley, Ron Harry's best friend. Ron is the sixth child in his family to attend Hogwarts, and like his siblings, he belongs to Gryffindor House. Ron is a tall, thin, gangly, freckle-faced redhead with big hands and feet and a long nose. He never gets anything new, but has to make do with hand-me-downs from his older brothers. Even his pet rat, Scabbers, used to belong to his brother Percy. Ron gets Scabbers when Percy gets an owl (Hermes) to acknowledge his appointment as a Hogwarts prefect. Ron is an avid quidditch fan and every inch of his bedroom at home is covered with posters of his favourite team, the Chudley Cannons. His favourite comic books are *The Adventures of Martin Miggs, The Mad Muggle*. When Ron was three, he broke his brother Fred's toy broomstick. Fred retaliated by turning Ron's teddy bear into a spider. Ron hasn't much liked spiders since.

Whomping Willow An extremely large and dangerous willow tree that protects itself by hitting out with its branches. Harry and Ron accidentally crash the Weasleys' flying car into the willow and barely escape with their lives.

Witch Weekly A popular magazine that has conferred its Most-Charming-Smile Award on the incompetent Gilderoy Lockhart five times in a row.

"Witching Hour" A popular radio show.

Wood, Oliver Captain and keeper for the Gryffindor quidditch team. Oliver is a burly youth who is four years ahead of Harry at Hogwarts.

You-Know-Who *See* **Voldemort**.

Autographs & Notes: